Contents

1 Cosmic Clay

The heart of stardust sculpting lies within the nebulae, those vast, swirling clouds of interstellar dust and gas. They are the cosmic clay, the raw material from which celestial wonders are born. Gathering this ethereal substance requires a delicate touch, an understanding of the subtle currents that flow through the cosmos. Imagine reaching out into the void, not with physical hands, but with focused intent, drawing strands of nebulae towards you, coaxing them to coalesce. This is not a brute force endeavor, but a dance, a harmonious interaction with the universe's breath. Different nebulae possess unique properties: some shimmer with vibrant hues, others glow with an internal luminescence. Some are dense and opaque, others wispy and translucent. Learning to discern these qualities is the first step towards mastering the art of nebula gathering. Consider the Orion Nebula, a vibrant stellar nursery teeming with nascent stars, or the Horsehead Nebula, a dark silhouette against a backdrop of glowing hydrogen. Each offers a distinct palette of colors and textures, a unique potential for artistic expression. Once gathered, the nebulae must be shaped. Void dust, those microscopic particles scattered throughout space, acts as a binding agent, a way to give form to the ethereal nebulae. Think of it as the scaffolding upon which you will build your celestial creation. Manipulating void dust requires precision, an understanding of its electrostatic properties. By carefully modulating energy fields, you can guide the dust particles, weaving them into intricate patterns, forming the skeletal structure of your sculpture. This process is akin to building with light, constructing forms from the very essence of the cosmos. The interplay of light and shadow becomes your primary tool, revealing and concealing, defining and suggesting.

The delicate structures formed from nebulae and void dust are ephemeral, prone to dissipation in the vastness of space. To give them permanence, they must undergo a process called celestial tempering. This involves harnessing the energy of nearby stars, carefully channeling their radiative output to fuse the dust and gas into a more stable form. Imagine bathing your sculpture in starlight, watching as the nebular clouds solidify, their colors deepening and intensifying. Celestial tempering is a delicate balance, requiring precise control over temperature and duration. Too much energy, and the delicate structure could vaporize. Too little, and it will remain fragile, susceptible to the forces of cosmic erosion. Mastering this process requires patience, a deep understanding of the interplay of energy and matter.

This process of celestial tempering isn't merely about hardening the nebulae and void dust. It's about imbuing them with new properties. The intense heat and radiation can trigger unique reactions within the cosmic clay, altering its color, texture, and even its luminescence. Imagine a sculpture forged from the heart of a supernova remnant, pulsating with the residual energy of the exploded star, or a piece crafted from the icy dust of a comet's tail, shimmering with an ethereal blue glow. The possibilities are as vast as the universe itself.

The act of gathering, shaping, and tempering cosmic clay is a deeply meditative practice, a way to connect with the fundamental forces of the universe. It is a conversation with the cosmos, a dance between the artist and the infinite. As you work with these ethereal materials, you begin to understand the interconnectedness of all things, the delicate balance that sustains creation. This understanding becomes embedded within your sculptures, transforming them from mere objects into expressions of cosmic harmony.

The tempered stardust, now a solidified medium, retains a subtle responsiveness to its surroundings. It can resonate with the energy of distant stars, its colors shifting and shimmering in response to celestial events. This dynamic quality adds another layer of complexity to the art, creating sculptures that are not static but ever-evolving, mirroring the constant flux of the universe. Imagine a sculpture that changes color with the phases of a nearby moon, or one that pulsates with the rhythm of a pulsar's beam. This responsiveness to the cosmos imbues the

artwork with a sense of aliveness, a connection to the greater whole.
Mastering the techniques of working with cosmic clay requires more than just skill and precision. It requires a deep understanding of the universe itself, its laws and principles, its rhythms and cycles. It is a journey of discovery, a continuous exploration of the infinite possibilities that lie within the stardust. Each nebula, each grain of void dust, holds a story, a whisper of cosmic history. By learning to listen to these whispers, by attuning ourselves to the language of the universe, we can unlock the true potential of cosmic clay, crafting wonders that transcend the limitations of our earthly imagination.

1.1 Gathering Nebulae

The universe offers a breathtaking palette of materials for the aspiring sculptor. For those seeking to craft wonders beyond the terrestrial, the nebulae, those vast clouds of gas and dust scattered across the cosmos, offer a unique and challenging medium. These celestial mists, birthplaces of stars, hold the raw ingredients for creations of extraordinary beauty and complexity. Gathering these nebular materials, however, is no simple task. It requires a deep understanding of their unique properties and a willingness to adapt to the unpredictable nature of the cosmos. Forget the earthly tools of chisel and mallet; here, the instruments are forces of gravity, magnetic fields, and the subtle push of stellar winds.
Consider the different types of nebulae, each with its own distinct characteristics. Emission nebulae, vibrant with the glow of ionized gas, offer luminous hues of red, blue, and violet, ideal for capturing the essence of celestial fire. Reflection nebulae, illuminated by nearby stars, shimmer with a softer, more ethereal light, lending themselves to works of delicate beauty and subtle shading. Dark nebulae, dense and opaque, can be incorporated to create dramatic contrasts and silhouettes against the backdrop of the cosmos. The very composition of a nebula – the ratio of hydrogen, helium, and heavier elements – affects its color, density, and how it interacts with surrounding energies. This knowledge is crucial for selecting the right nebular material for a specific artistic vision. Imagine sculpting with a material that shifts and changes under the influence of distant starlight, responding to the cosmic rhythm of the universe.

To gather these ephemeral substances requires a delicate touch. Imagine using carefully calibrated gravitational fields, almost like invisible nets, to draw the nebular material into a workable region of space. Magnetic fields, precisely manipulated, can act as guiding hands, shaping the raw nebula into initial forms. The subtle pressure of stellar winds can be harnessed to refine the gathered material, gently compressing it and increasing its density. This process demands patience and a deep understanding of the forces at play. It's not about brute force, but rather a delicate dance with the cosmic elements. Think of it as conducting a symphony of celestial forces, each instrument contributing to the final masterpiece.

One might employ specialized collectors, designed to navigate the turbulent currents within a nebula, filtering out specific elements or isotopes. These collectors, powered by the very energy they harvest, could be programmed to gather materials with specific spectral characteristics, allowing the artist to fine-tune the color and luminosity of their creations. Furthermore, imagine manipulating the temperature and pressure of the collected nebula, inducing phase changes within the dust and gas to create unique textures and properties. By carefully controlling these factors, an artist could coax a nebula into forming intricate crystalline structures, or weave it into delicate filaments of shimmering light.

The gathered nebulae, swirling and luminous, can then be stored within containment fields, ready to be shaped and sculpted. These fields, generated by carefully positioned emitters, prevent the gathered material from dissipating back into the vastness of space. They also provide a controlled environment where the artist can further refine the nebula's properties, preparing it for the next stage of the creative process. Within these fields, the nebula can be subjected to controlled bursts of energy, further enhancing its luminosity or inducing specific chemical reactions within the gas and dust. This careful preparation ensures that the nebula retains its vibrant colors and ethereal qualities, ready to be transformed into breathtaking works of art.

The challenge lies in maintaining the delicate balance between control and allowing the nebula to express its inherent nature. It's a conversation with the cosmos, a give and take that requires both artistic vision and scientific understanding.

This is the essence of gathering nebulae: a delicate dance between the artist and the universe, a partnership that gives birth to creations of unparalleled beauty and cosmic significance. The artist becomes a conductor of the cosmos, orchestrating the raw materials of creation into a symphony of light and form. This process is not merely about collecting material; it's about capturing the essence of the universe itself.

1.2 Shaping Void Dust

The very essence of void dust lies in its paradoxical nature: a nothingness that holds the potential for everything. It's not merely the absence of matter, but a primordial soup of latent energy, a whisper of existence waiting to be given form. Think of it as the sculptor's clay, yet far more ethereal, responsive to intention and imbued with a cosmic energy that vibrates with untold possibilities. To work with void dust is to engage in a dance with the universe itself, a subtle interplay of will and receptivity. Forget the rigid tools of earthly sculpture. Here, your instruments are focus, visualization, and the sheer power of creative intent.

Imagine reaching out, not with your hands, but with your mind, feeling the fine, almost imperceptible grains of void dust swirling around you. This isn't a physical touch, but a connection on a deeper, energetic level. Begin by gently coaxing the dust into a loose, nebulous cloud, a blank canvas upon which your vision will take shape. Feel its subtle resistance, its inherent tendency to disperse, and counter it with a gentle but firm resolve. This is the first step, the initial connection that establishes the dialogue between artist and medium. The key lies in understanding the subtle interplay of energies.

As you gather the void dust, visualize its transformation. Imagine the nebulous cloud coalescing, taking on a denser form, not through force, but through gentle persuasion. Picture the desired shape in your mind's eye with absolute clarity. The more defined your vision, the more readily the void dust will respond. This process demands patience and unwavering focus. It's a meditation in motion, a delicate balancing act between intention and allowing the material to express its inherent properties. Don't rush the process. Allow the form to emerge gradually, as if unfolding from within itself.

Now, consider the concept of density. Void dust, while seemingly insubstantial, possesses a spectrum of densities, each with its own unique characteristics. Imagine the difference between a wisp of smoke and a swirling nebula. Both are composed of particles, yet their density dictates their form and behavior. You can manipulate the density of void dust by focusing your intent. Imagine compressing the dust, drawing it tighter, increasing its solidity. This will create areas of greater definition and structure within your sculpture. Conversely, by loosening your focus, you can allow the dust to expand, creating ethereal, translucent areas that seem to shimmer with an inner light.

The interplay of density creates depth and dimension. It allows you to sculpt not just solid forms, but also the spaces between them, the voids that give shape and meaning to the whole. Think of a celestial landscape: the dense solidity of a nascent planet juxtaposed with the ethereal wisps of a nebula. This contrast, this interplay of presence and absence, is the very essence of sculpting with void dust. Experiment with varying degrees of density. Create areas of intense solidity and contrast them with areas of delicate translucence. Allow the light of distant stars to filter through your sculpture, revealing its inner structure and creating an interplay of light and shadow.

Remember that void dust is inherently responsive to light. It absorbs, reflects, and refracts light in ways that defy earthly physics. By manipulating the density of your sculpture, you can control how it interacts with light, creating stunning visual effects. Imagine a sculpture that appears solid from one angle, yet dissolves into shimmering mist when viewed from another. The possibilities are truly infinite. Explore the interplay of light and shadow. Use light to reveal the contours of your sculpture, to highlight its textures, and to create an ethereal glow that emanates from within.

Another critical aspect of working with void dust is the concept of resonance. Every particle of void dust vibrates with a subtle energy, a cosmic hum that connects it to the universe at large. By attuning your own energy to that of the void dust, you can establish a deeper connection, a resonance that enhances your ability to shape and mold the material. This requires a state of heightened awareness, a sensitivity to the subtle energies that permeate the cosmos. Practice quieting your mind, focusing your intention, and feeling the subtle vibrations of the void dust. As you deepen your connection with the void dust, you'll discover that it's not merely a passive material, but an active partner in the creative process. It will begin to respond to your thoughts and emotions, taking on forms that reflect your inner world. Embrace this collaborative aspect of stardust sculpting. Allow the void dust to guide you, to inspire you, and to reveal the hidden depths of your own creativity. This is the true magic of working with void dust: the ability to create not just physical forms, but expressions of the soul, imbued with the very essence of the cosmos. Allow your intuition to guide you. Experiment, explore, and allow the unexpected to unfold. The universe is your canvas, and void dust is your brush. What wonders will you create?

1.3 Celestial Tempering

Imagine the swirling chaos of a nebula, a celestial cloud of dust and gas, the raw material for your artistic endeavors. You've gathered it, shaped it, coaxed it into the desired form, but it remains volatile, ethereal. It needs substance, resilience. It needs tempering. Celestial tempering is not a single technique, but a collection of methods for solidifying and enhancing the stardust you've collected, transforming the ephemeral into the enduring. Think of it as the process of firing clay in a kiln, but on a cosmic scale, using the very energies of the universe.

One primary method utilizes focused starlight. By channeling the intense radiation from a star, you can superheat the stardust, fusing the particles together. This is a delicate process, akin to glassblowing. Too little heat and the stardust remains fragile, too much and it could vaporize entirely. The key is control, carefully modulating the starlight to achieve the desired density and consistency. The resulting material, once cooled, takes on a crystalline structure, shimmering with captured starlight. Its strength is remarkable, capable of withstanding the rigors of the cosmos.

Another approach involves harnessing the gravitational forces of celestial bodies. By carefully maneuvering large asteroids or even small moons, you can generate intense pressure within the stardust cloud. This compressive force, applied over vast periods, compacts and solidifies the material. The result is a substance with a unique granular texture, reminiscent of polished stone but possessing an otherworldly luminescence. This technique is particularly suited for creating large-scale sculptures, where immense strength and stability are required.

A more esoteric method utilizes the energy of quasars, the intensely bright cores of distant galaxies. By focusing their energy through intricate lensing systems made of meticulously arranged dark matter, you can imbue the stardust with unique properties. This technique is incredibly complex and requires a deep understanding of astrophysical principles. However, the rewards are immense. Quasar-tempered stardust takes on an almost ethereal quality, capable of holding and emitting light in mesmerizing patterns. This is ideal for creating sculptures that interact with light, casting shimmering shadows and illusions across the cosmos.

Beyond these primary methods, there are countless variations and combinations. Some artists prefer to temper their stardust using the intense magnetic fields of pulsars, imbuing their creations with a subtle, pulsating energy. Others harness the power of cosmic rays, creating materials that shift and change color over time. The possibilities are truly endless, limited only by your imagination and understanding of the universe.

The choice of tempering technique is intimately tied to the desired outcome. Are you crafting a delicate, light-filled sculpture? Starlight tempering might be the best approach. Do you envision a colossal, imposing structure? Gravitational compression could be the answer. Or perhaps you seek to capture the ephemeral essence of a nebula within a solid form. Then the esoteric arts of quasar tempering may be required.

Mastering celestial tempering takes time, patience, and a willingness to experiment. There will be failures, moments of frustration, times when your carefully crafted creation crumbles into dust. But each failure is a lesson learned, a step closer to understanding the intricate dance of cosmic forces. Embrace the challenges, for it is through these trials that you will truly become a sculptor of stardust.

As you gain experience, you will develop an intuitive understanding of the various tempering techniques. You will learn to read the subtle cues in the stardust, sensing its readiness for transformation. You will feel the flow of cosmic energies, guiding your hand as you shape and mold the raw material of the universe. And in time, your creations will transcend mere sculpture, becoming testaments to the boundless potential of artistic expression within the infinite canvas of the cosmos. This is the essence of sculpting with stardust: a journey of discovery, innovation, and the pursuit of artistic transcendence. Remember, the universe itself is your kiln, the stars your forge, and the endless expanse of space your gallery.

2 Ethereal Forms

Imagine capturing a whisper of light, holding it gently in your cosmic clay. This is the essence of working with ethereal forms, where we strive not to solidify, but to suggest. We build structures not of density, but of translucence, allowing the void to breathe through our creations. Think of the delicate tracery of a supernova remnant, its filaments of light stretching across the cosmos. This is the kind of ephemeral beauty we seek to emulate, capturing a fleeting moment in the vast expanse of time and space. Our medium is not stone, but the very fabric of the universe itself, woven into forms as delicate as a spider's silk, shimmering with captured starlight.

Now consider the concept of phantom textures. These are not textures you can touch, but those you perceive through the interplay of light and shadow. Think of the shimmering surface of a nebula, appearing smooth from afar, but revealing intricate layers of gas and dust upon closer inspection. We can recreate this effect by carefully manipulating the density of our cosmic clay, allowing light to penetrate to varying degrees. Imagine a sculpture that appears solid when viewed from one angle, yet dissolves into a hazy cloud when seen from another. This interplay of presence and absence is key to capturing the ethereal quality we seek. It's about crafting illusions, playing with the viewer's perception, and inviting them to complete the artwork with their own imagination.

Ephemeral sculptures are the epitome of this delicate art. These are not meant to last for eons, but to exist as fleeting moments of beauty, like a comet streaking across the night sky. Imagine a sculpture crafted from solidified moonlight, slowly melting away as dawn approaches. Or perhaps a swirling vortex of nebula dust, held together by a fragile web of starlight, destined to eventually dissipate back into the cosmos. This transience adds another layer of meaning to our work, reminding us of the impermanence of all things. It challenges us to appreciate the beauty of the moment, knowing that it will eventually fade away, leaving behind only a memory.

To create these ephemeral wonders, we must develop a deep understanding of light. It is our chisel, our brush, our primary tool. We learn to bend and shape it, to capture it within our sculptures, and to use it to reveal the hidden depths of our creations. Think of the way sunlight filters through a cloud, creating beams of light that illuminate the dust motes suspended within. We can mimic this effect by incorporating tiny particles of reflective material into our cosmic clay, allowing them to catch and scatter the light. This creates a sense of movement and life within the sculpture, giving it a shimmering, ethereal glow.

The manipulation of shadow is equally important. Shadows are not merely the absence of light, but rather a partner in the dance of creation. They define form, add depth, and create a sense of mystery. Imagine a sculpture that appears as a simple sphere when fully illuminated, but reveals intricate carvings and textures when partially obscured by shadow. This interplay of light and shadow adds a layer of complexity to our work, inviting the viewer to explore its hidden dimensions. It's about understanding the negative space, the voids, and how they interact with the light to create a complete artistic experience.

Finally, consider the importance of suggestion. In working with ethereal forms, we are not striving for photorealism, but rather for an evocation of the essence of a thing. Think of a wisp of smoke, barely visible against a dark background. We can capture its ephemeral quality by using translucent materials and carefully manipulating the light and shadow. We are not trying to recreate the smoke itself, but rather the feeling of its fleeting presence. This subtle approach allows us to create works that are both beautiful and evocative, inviting the viewer to engage with the artwork on a deeper, more emotional level.

Working with ethereal forms is a constant exploration of the boundaries of our medium. It's a dance between presence and absence, solidity and transparency, light and shadow. It challenges us to think beyond the tangible and embrace the ephemeral, to capture the fleeting beauty of the cosmos in our creations. By mastering these techniques, we can create works that transcend the physical realm and touch the very essence of the universe itself. Remember, it is not about replicating, but about evoking. Capture the whisper, the fleeting thought, the ephemeral dream, and hold it gently in your cosmic clay. Let the universe breathe through your creations.

2.1 Whispers of Light

Light, in its purest form, is the essence of ethereal sculpture. It breathes life into the void dust, transforming the mundane into the magnificent. Consider light not merely as illumination, but as a sculptural element itself, a tangible substance you can mold and manipulate. Think of capturing starlight within crystalline structures, refracting and diffusing it to create shimmering auras and iridescent glows. Experiment with prisms and lenses formed from solidified nebulae, bending and twisting rays of cosmic light into breathtaking displays. Imagine a sculpture that appears as a simple, dark form by day, but at night, pulses with internal light, revealing its intricate internal structure. This is the power of light as a sculpting medium.

This interaction between light and form creates the illusion of depth and dimension. Shadows become allies, not adversaries. They sculpt the unseen, hinting at forms just beyond perception, adding a layer of mystery and intrigue to your creations. A gentle curve, kissed by a fleeting beam of light, can appear to ripple and flow, while a strategically placed void can create the illusion of infinite depth. Mastering this interplay of light and shadow is key to crafting truly ethereal forms. Imagine a sculpture of a celestial flower, its petals crafted from translucent void dust, each vein glowing with captured starlight. The shadows cast by the petals create a sense of delicate fragility, enhancing the flower's otherworldly beauty.

Explore the concept of luminosity. Imbue your sculptures with an inner radiance, allowing them to emanate a soft, ethereal glow. This can be achieved by incorporating phosphorescent minerals gleaned from distant nebulae or by capturing and containing the faint luminescence of void dust itself. A sculpture that appears to emit its own light transcends the mundane, becoming a beacon of otherworldly beauty. Visualize a field of stardust flowers, each gently pulsating with an internal light, creating a mesmerizing landscape that shifts and changes with the subtle ebb and flow of cosmic energy.

Consider the transient nature of light. Its ephemeral quality can be harnessed to create sculptures that evolve and transform over time. Imagine a sculpture that relies on the changing angles of starlight to reveal different facets of its form, or one that fades and brightens with the waxing and waning of a nearby nebula's luminosity. By embracing the transient, you can create works of art that are never truly static, always in a state of becoming. Picture a swirling vortex of stardust, illuminated by a distant quasar. As the light shifts and changes, the vortex appears to expand and contract, revealing hidden depths and intricate patterns within its swirling form.

Texture plays a vital role in how light interacts with a sculpture. A smooth, polished surface will reflect light differently than a rough, textured one. Experiment with different techniques to create a variety of textures in your stardust creations. Perhaps you might carve intricate patterns into the surface of a solidified nebula, or create a sculpture with a surface as smooth and reflective as a still cosmic lake. Consider the way light dances across the surface of a newly formed planet, highlighting the rough texture of its nascent crust, and use this as inspiration for your own creations.

Don't be afraid to break free from traditional notions of form. Ethereal sculptures can be as fluid and amorphous as a nebula or as sharp and angular as a crystalline shard. Explore the possibilities of creating sculptures that seem to defy gravity, floating effortlessly in the void. Imagine a cascade of stardust, frozen mid-flow, each particle shimmering with captured starlight. The form is fluid and dynamic, yet possesses an ethereal grace that transcends its physical limitations.

Remember, the goal is not simply to create a beautiful object, but to evoke a feeling, to tell a story. What whispers does your sculpture convey? What secrets does it hold within its luminous form? Let your imagination soar, and allow your creativity to guide you as you sculpt with the very essence of light. Visualize a solitary figure crafted from shimmering void dust, its face tilted towards a distant nebula, as if listening to the whispers of the cosmos. The figure's posture conveys a sense of longing and wonder, inviting the viewer to contemplate the mysteries of the universe.

By mastering the interplay of light, shadow, luminosity, and texture, you can create ethereal sculptures that transcend the boundaries of the physical world, evoking a sense of wonder and awe in all who behold them. These are not mere objects, but whispers of light, tangible manifestations of the dreams and visions that dance within the sculptor's heart. They are portals to other realms, invitations to explore the infinite possibilities of the universe, and testaments to the boundless power of artistic expression. They stand as beacons of creativity, illuminating the path towards a deeper understanding of the cosmos and our place within its grand design. Let your hands be guided by the whispers of light, and let your creations illuminate the universe with their ethereal beauty.

2.2 Phantom Textures

The ethereal nature of stardust allows for the creation of textures unseen in terrestrial art. Think of the swirling patterns within a nebula, the delicate frost on a comet's tail, or the rough, pitted surface of an asteroid. These are the inspirations for phantom textures, sensations felt more than seen, implied rather than explicitly rendered. Imagine running your hand across a sculpture that seems smooth, yet evokes the sensation of a thousand tiny stars prickling your skin. This is the power of phantom texture – to create an experience that transcends the purely visual. We achieve this through subtle manipulations of the stardust medium.

Consider the delicate interplay of light and shadow. By carefully etching microscopic grooves onto the surface of your sculpture, you can create patterns that only reveal themselves when light catches them at specific angles. These patterns, almost invisible in direct light, can shimmer and shift as the viewer moves, creating the illusion of movement and depth. This technique can be used to evoke the sensation of wind rippling across a field of stardust, or the slow, creeping flow of a nebula. Experiment with varying depths and angles of these grooves to achieve a wide range of tactile illusions.

The density of the stardust itself can also play a crucial role in creating phantom textures. Imagine a sculpture composed of loosely packed stardust particles. When touched, it might give way slightly, creating a sensation of softness and yielding. Conversely, a densely packed area can feel firm and resistant. By combining these variations in density, you can create complex tactile landscapes within a single sculpture. Think of a celestial flower, its petals soft and yielding, while its stem remains firm and supportive.

Temperature manipulation adds another layer to this sensory experience. By subtly altering the temperature of specific areas on your sculpture, you can evoke sensations of warmth or coolness. Imagine a sculpture of a comet, its icy tail radiating a faint chill, while its head, warmed by the distant sun, emits a gentle warmth. This contrast in temperature can add a powerful dimension to your phantom textures, further blurring the lines between the visual and the tactile.

Don't limit yourself to the purely physical. Incorporate elements of luminescence into your phantom textures. Imagine a sculpture that seems smooth to the touch, yet glows faintly from within, creating the illusion of a hidden energy source. This internal light can be achieved by embedding small, luminescent stardust particles within the denser areas of your sculpture. The effect is subtle, yet powerful, adding a sense of mystery and intrigue to your work.

Explore the use of magnetic fields to interact with your stardust sculptures. By embedding magnetic particles within the stardust, you can create areas that subtly repel or attract other magnetic objects. Imagine a sculpture that seems to gently push away your hand as you approach it, or one that draws your fingers towards specific points on its surface. This interactive element adds a dynamic quality to your phantom textures, encouraging viewers to engage with your work in a more profound way.

Sound can also play a crucial role in creating phantom textures. By incorporating miniature sonic resonators within your sculpture, you can create subtle vibrations that are felt rather than heard. Imagine a sculpture that emits a low hum when touched, or one that vibrates in response to changes in light intensity. These subtle vibrations can add another layer of sensory information, further enhancing the tactile experience of your work.

Think about the contrast between smooth and rough textures. Imagine a sculpture that appears smooth from a distance, yet reveals a rough, granular texture upon closer inspection. This contrast can be achieved by layering different densities of stardust, creating a sense of depth and complexity. Consider the surface of a distant moon, seemingly smooth when viewed through a telescope, yet revealed to be a landscape of craters and mountains upon closer examination.

Experiment with the illusion of weight. By manipulating the density and distribution of stardust within your sculpture, you can create the impression of weight or weightlessness. Imagine a sculpture that appears heavy and substantial, yet floats effortlessly in space. This interplay between visual expectation and tactile reality can create a powerful and disorienting effect, challenging the viewer's perception of the physical world.

Finally, remember that phantom textures are about creating an experience. Don't be afraid to push the boundaries of what is considered traditional sculpture. Embrace the ethereal nature of stardust and let your imagination guide you. The universe is full of inspiration; let it flow through you and manifest in your work. By mastering the art of phantom textures, you can create truly otherworldly wonders that will captivate and intrigue viewers for eons to come.

2.3 Ephemeral Sculptures

The essence of ephemeral sculpture lies in its transience. It is a dance with time, a fleeting moment captured in the swirling dust of nebulae and the fading glow of starlight. Unlike carving mountains or shaping clay, working with these ethereal materials demands a different approach, a surrender to the impermanence of the cosmos. Think of a whisper of wind shaping a sand dune, constantly shifting, reforming, never truly fixed. This is the spirit we must embrace when crafting sculptures that are destined to dissolve back into the void.

Consider the medium itself. We're not dealing with solid stone or metal, but with the very fabric of space. Nebulae, those vast clouds of gas and dust, are our clay. We gather them, coax them into form using the subtle forces of gravity and light. Imagine using magnetic fields to gently pull strands of luminescent gas into swirling patterns, like a celestial kaleidoscope. Or perhaps harnessing the energy of solar winds to sculpt shimmering curtains of stardust, ever-changing with the

celestial currents. The possibilities are as vast as the universe itself.
One technique involves harnessing the faint luminescence within nebulae. By carefully manipulating the density and composition of the gas clouds, we can create pockets of light and shadow, forming three-dimensional images that shift and shimmer with an ethereal glow. Picture a ghostly figure emerging from a nebula, its form defined by the interplay of light and darkness. It exists only for a moment, a fleeting apparition in the cosmic ballet. This requires an understanding of the unique properties of each nebula. Some are rich in metallic dust, offering a brilliant, reflective surface. Others are composed primarily of hydrogen and helium, glowing with a soft, diffused light. Learning to read these subtle differences is key to creating ephemeral sculptures that resonate with the inherent beauty of the cosmos.
This delicate manipulation of light requires precision and patience. Think of it as painting with starlight, using the subtle gradations of luminosity to define form and create depth. Imagine weaving threads of light through the darkness, crafting intricate patterns that appear to float in the void. The ephemeral nature of the medium demands a different mindset. We're not striving for permanence, but rather celebrating the fleeting beauty of the moment.
Consider the lifespan of your creation. Will it be a fleeting spectacle, lasting only a few moments before dissolving back into the nebula? Or will it be a more enduring piece, gradually evolving over centuries as the celestial currents reshape its form? This understanding of time is crucial to the art of ephemeral sculpture. It allows us to create works that resonate with the grand cycles of creation and destruction that govern the universe.
The very act of creation, in this context, becomes a meditation on impermanence. We learn to let go of the need for control, embracing the unpredictable nature of the cosmos. Imagine a sculpture formed from the trails of comets, its shape constantly evolving as the icy bodies streak across the sky. It's a reminder that beauty can be found even in the most transient of forms. This is the heart of ephemeral sculpture: a celebration of the fleeting, a testament to the ever-changing nature of the universe.
Creating ephemeral sculptures also involves an understanding of the surround-

ing environment. The gravitational pull of nearby stars, the flow of interstellar dust, even the subtle pressure of light can all influence the shape and lifespan of your creation. Think of placing a sculpture within the heart of a nebula, where it will be bathed in the swirling energies of the cosmos. Or perhaps positioning it near a black hole, where its form will be distorted by the immense gravitational forces.

Remember, the key is to work with the universe, not against it. Allow the natural forces of the cosmos to shape your creations, adding a layer of serendipity to the artistic process. Imagine a sculpture formed from the swirling dust around a newborn star, its shape constantly evolving as the stellar winds push and pull the material. It's a collaboration between the artist and the universe, a dance between intention and chance.

Finally, consider the emotional impact of your ephemeral sculpture. What message do you wish to convey with this fleeting creation? Is it a celebration of the beauty of the cosmos? A meditation on the transient nature of existence? Or perhaps a simple expression of wonder and awe? Imagine a sculpture that slowly fades away, leaving behind only a faint shimmer in the void. It's a poignant reminder of the ephemeral nature of all things, a call to appreciate the beauty of the present moment. This is the power of ephemeral sculpture: to connect us with the vastness of the universe and the fleeting beauty of existence.

3 Stellar Gardens

The act of planting starseeds is not a casual scattering, but a precise and delicate art. Each seed, a condensed fragment of nebulae, pulsates with potential. They are not merely planted; they are woven into the fabric of the sculpted landscapes, nestled within the curves of void dust formations and tucked into the crevices of celestial tempering. Consider the gravitational pull of your sculpted environment. Where will nascent starlight gather? Where will the cosmic winds deposit ethereal nutrients? Understanding these flows is crucial to successful starseed placement. A misplaced seed will wither, failing to draw upon the ambient energies needed to bloom. A well-placed seed, however, will flourish, drawing upon the sculpted landscape's inherent energy and transforming it into vibrant, otherworldly life.

Think of your stellar garden as a living sculpture, constantly evolving. The initial placement of starseeds is just the first brushstroke on a canvas of infinite potential. As your starseeds germinate and grow, they will interact with their surroundings, shaping and being shaped by the landscape. This dynamic interplay creates a self-sustaining ecosystem within your sculpture, a microcosm of the universe itself. Observe the subtle shifts in starlight, the gentle pulsations of energy, and the way newborn nebulae intertwine with existing formations. These are the whispers of your garden's evolution, a language you must learn to understand and nurture. Embrace the unpredictable nature of this process, allowing the garden to guide your artistic hand.

Lunar blooms possess a unique and ethereal beauty, unlike anything found in terrestrial gardens. Bathed in the reflected light of distant suns and nurtured by the subtle energies of the moon's core, these otherworldly flora exhibit a spectrum of luminescence and form. Their petals, woven from solidified moonlight and infused with captured starlight, unfold in intricate patterns, radiating a soft, otherworldly glow. Some resemble crystalline orchids, their translucent petals shimmering with trapped starlight. Others mimic bioluminescent fungi, casting an eerie, pulsating light across the lunar surface. Each bloom is a testament to the unique conditions of its environment, a living sculpture shaped by the moon's gentle touch.

Cultivating lunar blooms requires a deep understanding of their specific needs. They thrive in the cool, shadowed craters of the moon, drawing sustenance from the mineral-rich regolith. Unlike terrestrial plants that require soil and sunlight, lunar blooms draw energy directly from the moon's core, channeling its subtle vibrations into vibrant life. The composition of the regolith is crucial. A balance of minerals, including silicon, titanium, and aluminum, is essential for their growth. Too much iron, for example, can stifle their luminescence, while a deficiency in calcium can weaken their delicate structures. Experiment with different blends of regolith, observing the subtle changes in the blooms' color, luminosity, and growth patterns.

Consider the interplay of light and shadow within your lunar garden. While some blooms thrive in the deepest shadows, others require a delicate balance of darkness and reflected sunlight. The angle of incidence, the intensity of the reflected light, and the duration of exposure all play a crucial role in their development. Strategically placing reflective surfaces, such as polished obsidian or crystalline structures, can channel and redirect light, creating microclimates within your garden. This careful manipulation of light and shadow will not only enhance the aesthetic beauty of your blooms but also influence their growth patterns and luminescence.

The arrangement of your lunar blooms is an art in itself. Think of the overall composition, the interplay of colors, and the flow of energy within the garden. Cluster similar blooms together to create pools of vibrant color, or scatter them across the landscape to mimic the natural randomness of a lunar meadow. Experiment with different heights and textures, intertwining trailing vines with towering crystalline flowers to create a sense of depth and complexity. Consider the narrative you wish to convey with your garden. Is it a tranquil oasis of ethereal beauty, or a dynamic ecosystem teeming with life? Let your artistic vision guide your hand, allowing the unique characteristics of each bloom to contribute to the overall narrative. The art of cultivating a lunar bloom is a constant dance between control and surrender, a delicate balance between scientific precision and artistic intuition. Embrace the unpredictable nature of this process, allowing the lunar environment to shape your creations and guide your hand. In doing so, you will unlock the hidden potential of these ethereal flora, creating gardens of unparalleled beauty and wonder.

3.1 Planting Starseeds

Imagine the void as your canvas. Not a flat, two-dimensional surface, but an endless, three-dimensional expanse brimming with potential. Within this void, we'll cultivate our Stellar Gardens, beginning with the careful placement of starseeds. These aren't seeds in the terrestrial sense, but concentrated pockets of nebulae, imbued with the potential for stellar growth. Think of them as the embryonic hearts of future suns, miniature nebulae swirling with nascent energy. Your task is to select these seeds, each a unique cocktail of cosmic dust and energy, and place them within the sculpted landscapes you've crafted. This process demands careful consideration of placement. The proximity of other celestial bodies, the density of surrounding nebulae, and the flow of cosmic energies all influence a starseed's development.

Consider the desired outcome. Do you envision a blazing blue giant, its intense radiation sculpting the surrounding nebulae into fantastical formations? Or perhaps a cluster of red dwarfs, their gentle glow illuminating a field of ethereal flora? The type of starseed you choose, its placement, and the environment you cultivate around it will dictate the final result. This process isn't about imposing your will upon the cosmos, but rather about understanding and guiding its inherent energies. It's a delicate dance between artistic vision and the natural laws of the universe. Observe the interplay of forces within your garden, the gravitational pulls and energetic currents that shape its evolution. Adjust your approach as needed, nurturing the growth of your stellar seedlings with patience and precision.

Now, let's delve into the specifics of starseed selection. Nebulae, the birthplaces of stars, come in a vast array of compositions. Some are rich in hydrogen, the fuel of stellar fusion, while others are dense with heavier elements forged in the hearts of dying stars. This compositional variety translates into a diverse palette of starseed possibilities. For example, a nebula rich in iron might yield a star with a distinctive reddish hue, while one abundant in silicon could give rise to a star that emits a soft, ethereal glow. Study the spectral signature of each nebula, the unique fingerprint of its elemental makeup. This information will guide your selection, allowing you to choose starseeds that align with your artistic vision.

Once you've chosen your starseeds, the next step is planting. This isn't a matter of simply scattering them across the void. Each seed requires a carefully prepared environment to flourish. Consider the density of the surrounding nebulae. Too dense, and the seed might be suffocated, its growth stunted. Too sparse, and it might lack the nourishment needed to ignite. The gravitational influence of nearby celestial bodies also plays a crucial role. A strategically placed black hole, for example, could act as a cosmic sculptor, its immense gravity warping the surrounding nebulae into dramatic swirls and spirals.

As your starseeds mature, they'll begin to exert their own influence on the surrounding environment. Their radiation will sculpt the nebulae, creating intricate patterns of light and shadow. Their gravitational fields will attract and repel other celestial bodies, setting them in motion within your Stellar Garden. This dynamic interplay of forces is what brings your creation to life, transforming it from a static sculpture into a vibrant, evolving ecosystem. Embrace this dynamism, allowing the universe to become your collaborator. Observe the unfolding cosmic dance, and adjust your approach as needed, nurturing the growth of your stellar seedlings with a delicate touch.

Remember, patience is key. The growth of a star is a cosmic timescale event, unfolding over eons. Don't expect immediate results. Instead, cultivate a mindset of observation and adaptation. Watch as your starseeds slowly ignite, their light gradually illuminating the surrounding void. Observe the interplay of forces within your garden, the gravitational pulls and energetic currents that shape its evolution. This long-term perspective will allow you to appreciate the grand scale of your creation, the slow but steady unfolding of cosmic processes. It's a testament to the power of patience and the enduring beauty of the universe.

Finally, consider the interplay of light and shadow within your garden. The brilliant light of a newly formed star can cast long, dramatic shadows across the surrounding nebulae, creating an ethereal landscape of contrasting light and darkness. Experiment with different placements and combinations of stars to achieve a desired effect. Perhaps you envision a field of dim red dwarfs, their gentle glow illuminating a field of phosphorescent nebulae. Or maybe you prefer the dramatic contrast of a single, blazing blue giant, its intense radiation carving intricate patterns in the surrounding cosmic dust. The possibilities are as vast as the universe itself.

In creating Stellar Gardens, you're not just sculpting with stardust, you're cultivating life, nurturing the growth of celestial ecosystems. It's a process of collaboration with the cosmos, a dance between artistic vision and the inherent forces of the universe. Embrace this interplay, and watch as your creations bloom into wonders of otherworldly beauty. Remember the delicate balance between intention and allowance. Guide the growth of your garden, but also allow space for the unexpected, for the serendipitous discoveries that arise from the chaotic dance of creation. This is the art of sculpting with stardust: not just creating, but cultivating, nurturing, and becoming a part of the cosmic symphony.

3.2 Lunar Bloom

The ethereal glow of lunar flora is unlike anything found on terrestrial terrains. It pulses with an inner luminescence, a soft, cool light that seems to emanate from the very core of the plant. This luminescence is not merely decorative; it's the lifeblood of these unique organisms, a testament to their adaptation to the moon's specific conditions. Harnessing this inherent light is key to cultivating thriving lunar gardens. Consider the placement of each plant in relation to the ambient starlight and the shadows cast by larger stardust formations. These subtle interactions of light and shadow will dramatically impact the overall aesthetic of your lunar bloom.

Begin by visualizing the lunar landscape you wish to cultivate. Is it a tranquil, moonlit meadow of softly swaying luminous grasses? Or perhaps a vibrant, otherworldly garden teeming with bioluminescent flowers in a spectrum of impossible hues? The possibilities are as limitless as the cosmos themselves. Once you have a clear vision, you can begin selecting the appropriate lunar flora. Consider the texture, color, and intensity of their luminescence. A harmonious blend of these elements will create a captivating and otherworldly display.

Manipulating the stardust soil itself is crucial for successful lunar gardening. The soil's composition directly affects the vibrancy and health of your lunar blooms. Infuse the stardust with varying concentrations of captured starlight, experimenting with different levels of luminosity. This careful calibration of light within the soil will nourish the delicate root systems of the lunar plants and enhance their ethereal glow. Remember, the moon's surface experiences extreme temperature fluctuations, therefore, a stable, light-infused soil provides essential thermal regulation for these delicate organisms.

Observe the natural growth patterns of your chosen lunar flora. Some species thrive in clusters, their luminescence intertwining to create a mesmerizing tapestry of light. Others prefer solitude, their individual brilliance standing out against the backdrop of the lunar landscape. Understanding these nuances will guide your planting strategy, allowing you to create a dynamic and visually stunning composition. Experiment with different arrangements, allowing the natural beauty of each plant to complement the others. The interplay of these luminous forms will add depth and intrigue to your lunar garden.

As your lunar garden flourishes, consider incorporating elements of movement. Gentle lunar breezes, created by carefully manipulating the surrounding void dust, can cause the luminous flora to sway and dance, creating a captivating display of light and motion. This subtle animation will bring your lunar garden to life, imbuing it with a sense of otherworldly tranquility. The interplay of light, shadow, and movement will create a truly mesmerizing experience for the viewer.

To further enhance the otherworldly beauty of your lunar blooms, experiment with different methods of refracting and reflecting light. Introduce crystalline stardust formations, strategically placed to capture and scatter the ambient starlight. These crystalline structures will act as prisms, casting rainbows of ethereal light across your lunar garden. The interplay of these refracted colors will add a touch of magic to the already enchanting landscape.

Think beyond individual plants and consider the overall ecosystem you're creating. Introduce elements of contrast and surprise. Plant a cluster of deep violet luminescent fungi at the base of a towering, silver-leaved stardust tree. The contrasting colors and textures will create a focal point, drawing the viewer's eye and sparking their imagination. These unexpected combinations will add a sense of wonder and discovery to your lunar garden.

Cultivating lunar blooms is not merely about planting seeds; it's about sculpting with light itself. It's about understanding the delicate balance between shadow and illumination, movement and stillness, color and texture. It's about creating a living, breathing ecosystem that radiates with an otherworldly beauty. Embrace the unique challenges and endless possibilities of this ethereal art form, and your lunar garden will flourish with a breathtaking luminescence. Remember that each element, from the smallest flower to the largest stardust formation, contributes to the overall harmony and beauty of your lunar creation. The careful interplay of these elements will transform your lunar garden into a true masterpiece of stardust sculpting. As you continue to experiment and refine your techniques, you will discover new and exciting ways to manipulate light and create truly breathtaking lunar blooms. The moon's surface becomes your canvas, and stardust, your medium. With each new creation, you'll push the boundaries of what's possible, crafting ethereal landscapes that inspire wonder and awe.

Consider the lifecycle of your chosen flora. Some lunar blooms may exhibit a pulsating luminescence, their light intensifying and diminishing in a rhythmic cycle. Others may gradually change color over time, creating a shifting tapestry of hues across your lunar garden. These dynamic elements will add a layer of complexity and intrigue to your creation. Observing and understanding these natural rhythms will allow you to orchestrate a captivating display of light and color that evolves over time.

Finally, remember that cultivating a lunar garden is a continuous process of learning and experimentation. Embrace the unexpected. Don't be afraid to try new combinations of flora, to experiment with different soil compositions, or to manipulate the light in unconventional ways. It is through this constant exploration that you will discover new and innovative techniques, pushing the boundaries of stardust sculpting and creating truly unique and breathtaking lunar blooms. The lunar surface awaits your creative touch, an infinite canvas upon which to paint with light and life.

4 Astral Creatures

The breath of creation stirs within the sculptor's hands, ready to mold not still life, but vibrant, ethereal beings. To sculpt an Astral Creature is to weave together stardust and dreams, to breathe life into the void. Consider the Cosmic Leviathan, a creature of immense scale, its form undulating through the nebular seas. Its creation begins with a core of densely packed void dust, tempered with the fires of nascent stars. Layer upon layer, the sculptor adds to this core, shaping the Leviathan's colossal form, hinting at the powerful muscles beneath its shimmering skin. The final touch, perhaps, is the embedding of luminescent starseeds along its flanks, mimicking the bioluminescence of deep-sea creatures, creating an ethereal glow that illuminates its passage through the cosmic darkness.
Nebula Nymphs, in stark contrast to the Leviathan's grandeur, are beings of delicate grace. Their forms are less defined, shimmering clouds of stardust shaped by whispers of light. To craft a Nebula Nymph, the sculptor must embrace a gentler touch. Wisps of nebulae are gathered, their iridescent hues blended with subtle manipulations of light and shadow. The form is suggested rather than explicitly stated, a fleeting glimpse of a dancer caught mid-twirl. The magic lies in the illusion, the ephemeral nature of their existence, a reminder of the transient beauty of the cosmos. Their existence is a dance, a fleeting moment captured in stardust.
Solar Serpents, creatures of pure energy, present a unique challenge. Their bodies are forged from the very essence of starlight, captured and woven into sinuous forms. The sculptor must work with intense focus, channeling the raw power of the sun. Imagine threads of sunlight, pulled and twisted into intricate knots, forming the serpent's scales. Each scale must be carefully aligned, creating a

flow of energy that ripples along the serpent's body. The final touch is the serpent's eyes, two miniature suns blazing with captured starlight, a testament to the sculptor's mastery over celestial energies. Their sinuous forms writhe across the canvas of space, leaving trails of shimmering light.

Then we have the Asteroid Antelope, a creature of surprising elegance. Forged from the remnants of shattered asteroids, these creatures embody the resilience of life in the harsh vacuum of space. The sculptor must carefully select fragments of asteroid, each piece chosen for its unique texture and color. These fragments are then bound together, not with void dust, but with threads of solidified starlight, creating a network of glowing veins that hold the creature together. The challenge lies in balancing the ruggedness of the asteroid fragments with the ethereal glow of the starlight, creating a creature that is both strong and beautiful. Their hooves strike sparks from the cosmic dust, leaving a trail of shimmering light in their wake.

Finally, the Void Wraith, a creature shrouded in mystery. Unlike the other Astral Creatures, the Wraith is not sculpted from stardust, but from the very absence of it. It is a creature of pure shadow, a void within the void. To create a Void Wraith, the sculptor must work with the darkness itself, manipulating the shadows between the stars. The Wraith's form is constantly shifting, a swirling vortex of nothingness that seems to defy the laws of physics. Its presence is felt more than seen, a chilling reminder of the vast emptiness that permeates the universe. Their ethereal whispers echo through the void, a haunting reminder of the mysteries that lie beyond our comprehension. The creation of a Void Wraith is a delicate dance with nothingness, a testament to the sculptor's ability to find form within the formless. They are the embodiment of the unknown, a constant reminder of the vastness and mystery of the cosmos. Each of these creatures, distinct in their form and essence, offers a unique exploration into the art of sculpting with stardust, inviting the artist to delve into the boundless possibilities of the celestial canvas.

4.1 Cosmic Leviathan

The Cosmic Leviathan, a creature of nebulae and void dust, represents a pinnacle achievement in stardust sculpting. Imagine a being of colossal proportions, its form swirling with the colors of nascent stars, drifting through the cosmic void. Its scales shimmer with captured starlight, each one a miniature nebula, pulsating with an inner light. Crafting such a majestic being requires a deep understanding of the principles outlined in the 'Cosmic Clay' section – gathering, shaping, and tempering the ethereal substance of nebulae. The process begins with the careful selection of nebulaic material, choosing hues and densities that will best capture the Leviathan's otherworldly essence.

Think of the Leviathan's form as a symphony of swirling nebulae. Rather than a rigid structure, envision layers of gathered nebulae, each layer contributing to the creature's immense form. Manipulate the void dust within these layers to create flowing, organic shapes, suggesting the powerful muscles beneath its shimmering skin. Remember the techniques of celestial tempering to solidify these ephemeral substances, giving the Leviathan a semblance of permanence amidst the ever-shifting cosmos. Imagine the subtle interplay of light and shadow across its vast form, creating an illusion of depth and movement.

The Leviathan's scales present a unique challenge, each one a microcosm of the larger sculpting process. Begin by shaping small pockets of condensed nebulae, imbuing them with a radiant inner glow. Experiment with different densities of void dust to create variations in color and luminosity, mimicking the natural variations found within real nebulae. Temper these miniature nebulae to a point where they hold their shape, yet retain a sense of ethereal fluidity. Attach these scales to the Leviathan's form, overlapping them like celestial armor, creating a breathtaking tapestry of light and color.

Consider the Leviathan's eyes, windows into its cosmic soul. Craft them from highly concentrated nebulae, giving them a piercing intensity. Imagine the swirling patterns within these eyes, hinting at the ancient wisdom and power contained within this magnificent creature. Surround the eyes with delicate wisps of void dust, creating an ethereal frame that further enhances their otherworldly gaze.

The Leviathan's movement is a dance of cosmic grace. Employ subtle gradations in the density of the surrounding nebulae to suggest the gentle currents that propel it through the void. Imagine the trailing wisps of stardust, remnants of its passage through the cosmos, adding to its aura of majestic serenity.

The creation of a Cosmic Leviathan is not merely an act of sculpting; it's an act of creation on a cosmic scale. It's about harnessing the raw power of the universe and shaping it into a form of breathtaking beauty and awe-inspiring grandeur. Think of the Leviathan as a living testament to the boundless potential of stardust sculpting, a symbol of the artist's ability to transform the ephemeral into the eternal.

Remember, the true beauty of the Leviathan lies not just in its physical form, but in the story it tells. It's a story of cosmic creation, of the artist's journey through the infinite canvas of the universe. It's a story that speaks to the deepest desires of the human heart, the yearning to connect with something larger than ourselves, to touch the very fabric of existence.

As you sculpt your Leviathan, allow your intuition to guide you. Embrace the unpredictable nature of the cosmic medium, allowing for serendipitous discoveries and unexpected turns. Let the Leviathan's form evolve organically, reflecting the ever-shifting nature of the cosmos itself.

Don't be afraid to experiment with different techniques, pushing the boundaries of what's possible with stardust sculpting. The creation of a Cosmic Leviathan is a journey of discovery, a process of continuous learning and growth.

Finally, remember that the Leviathan is not just a sculpture; it's an extension of your own artistic vision. It's a reflection of your unique understanding of the cosmos, your personal interpretation of the infinite possibilities that lie within the realm of stardust. Pour your heart and soul into its creation, and the Leviathan will become a living testament to your artistic passion and boundless creativity. It will be a masterpiece that will inspire awe and wonder for eons to come, a beacon of artistic brilliance shining brightly in the vast expanse of the cosmos.

4.2 Nebula Nymphs

Nebula Nymphs are among the most delicate and challenging creations a stardust sculptor can attempt. Their forms, ephemeral and shimmering, embody the very essence of nebulae – vast clouds of interstellar dust and gas. Capturing this ethereal nature requires a deep understanding of manipulating light, shadow, and the subtle interplay of color within the stardust medium. Unlike the more solid forms of the Cosmic Leviathan or the Asteroid Antelope, Nebula Nymphs rely on suggestion and illusion. Their bodies are not fully formed, but rather hinted at through swirling veils of color and light.

Begin by gathering the finest nebula dust, the kind that shimmers with iridescent hues. This dust, collected from the heart of vibrant nebulae, holds the key to capturing the Nymphs' luminescent qualities. Remember the lessons of Celestial Tempering, applying just enough heat and pressure to bind the dust particles without sacrificing their inherent luminosity. The goal is to create a material that can hold a semblance of form while still allowing light to pass through, creating an ethereal glow. Think of it as weaving a fabric of light, where the threads are strands of stardust.

The Nymph's form itself is an exercise in capturing movement and fluidity. Avoid hard lines and defined edges. Instead, strive to create a sense of flowing motion, as if the Nymph is constantly shifting and reforming within the nebula's embrace. This can be achieved by delicately layering the tempered stardust, allowing each layer to partially obscure the one beneath it, creating depth and a sense of movement. Imagine the gentle currents within a nebula, the slow, swirling dance of cosmic dust and gas. Let these movements inform your sculpting, allowing the Nymph's form to emerge organically, as if born from the nebula itself.

Color is crucial in capturing the Nymph's otherworldly beauty. Nebulae come in a breathtaking array of colors, from the fiery reds of hydrogen gas to the cool blues of oxygen and the vibrant purples of newly forming stars. Use these colors to imbue your Nymph with a sense of life and energy. Blend different shades of stardust, allowing them to merge and swirl like the nebula itself. Consider the emotional impact of different colors. Warm hues can evoke a sense of joy and vitality, while cooler tones can suggest mystery and tranquility.

The play of light and shadow is essential to creating the illusion of form. While the Nymph's body is largely translucent, carefully placed shadows can suggest the contours of her figure and create a sense of depth. This can be achieved by varying the density of the stardust, allowing light to pass through some areas more easily than others. Think of a wisp of smoke, how it catches the light in certain places, revealing its form through subtle variations in opacity. Apply this same principle to your sculpting, using light and shadow to define the Nymph's ethereal form.

A key element of the Nebula Nymph is its wings. These delicate appendages, crafted from the finest threads of stardust, should evoke a sense of lightness and grace. They should appear almost weightless, as if they are constantly catching the light and shifting in the nebula's gentle currents. Use long, flowing lines to create the wings, allowing them to trail behind the Nymph like wisps of smoke. Consider incorporating iridescent materials into the wings to enhance their shimmering quality, catching the light and reflecting it back in a dazzling display.

Integrating luminescent elements within the Nymph's form can further enhance its ethereal nature. Tiny fragments of captured starlight, woven into the stardust fabric, can create points of intense brightness, mimicking the sparkle of distant stars within a nebula. These points of light can be strategically placed to highlight certain features of the Nymph's form, drawing the viewer's eye and adding another layer of depth and complexity. Imagine the Nymph drifting through the nebula, her form illuminated by the faint glow of distant stars. Let this image guide your placement of the luminescent elements, creating a sense of wonder and magic.

Finally, remember that the Nebula Nymph is more than just a sculpture; it is an embodiment of the nebula itself. It is a fleeting moment of beauty, captured in stardust and light. Embrace the ephemeral nature of your creation, allowing it to evoke a sense of wonder and mystery. The true beauty of a Nebula Nymph lies in its fragility and its fleeting nature, a reminder of the constant change and evolution that characterizes the universe itself. Through careful manipulation of light, color, and shadow, you can create a truly otherworldly wonder, a testament to the infinite creative potential that lies within the stardust of the cosmos.

Consider the surrounding environment when displaying your Nebula Nymph. A darkened room, lit only by the faint glow of other stardust creations, can enhance the Nymph's ethereal beauty and create a truly immersive experience.

4.3 Solar Serpents

Imagine the sun, not as a blinding disc, but as a writhing, incandescent serpent, scales of plasma flickering and coiling across the cosmic canvas. Solar Serpents, beings of pure stellar energy, are among the most challenging yet rewarding astral creatures to sculpt. Capturing their dynamic form and inherent power requires a deep understanding of manipulating energized stardust and harnessing the forces of celestial tempering learned earlier. Begin by gathering a core of condensed solar flare material. This acts as the serpent's heart, a pulsating source of energy that will animate your creation.

This core must be carefully cooled and compressed, using the techniques described in the "Celestial Tempering" chapter. Remember the importance of maintaining a balance between heat and pressure. Too much heat, and the core will dissipate back into the solar winds. Too much pressure, and it will collapse into a dense, inert mass, losing the vibrant energy essential for a Solar Serpent. Once the core has reached a stable, molten state, begin to draw out strands of the material, shaping them into the serpentine body. Visualize the flow of energy within a real serpent, the way its muscles ripple beneath its skin. Mimic this flow in your sculpture, creating curves and coils that suggest movement even in stillness.

The scales of a Solar Serpent are not mere adornments; they are intricate collectors and radiators of solar energy. To create them, you'll need to work with smaller, more intensely heated fragments of solar flare. Shape these fragments into thin, overlapping plates, each one subtly angled to catch and reflect the light. The arrangement of these scales is crucial. Consider the way light plays across a serpent's scales in the physical world, creating an illusion of shimmering movement. Replicate this effect by carefully positioning each scale, ensuring that it both contributes to the overall form of the serpent and captures the light in a unique and dynamic way. Think of each scale as a miniature lens, focusing and amplifying the serpent's inner fire.

The eyes of a Solar Serpent are perhaps the most critical element. They are windows into the immense power contained within. Use small, perfectly spherical orbs of solidified starlight, imbued with a touch of nebulae for depth and luminescence. Position them carefully, angling them slightly to create a sense of alertness and predatory focus. The subtle glow emanating from these eyes will give your serpent an aura of both wisdom and danger. Imagine the gaze of a Solar Serpent meeting your own across the vastness of space, a silent acknowledgment of shared cosmic power.

The final stage is imbuing your Solar Serpent with movement. This isn't about physical animation; it's about creating the illusion of perpetual motion, the suggestion of coiled power ready to be unleashed. Achieve this by carefully manipulating the flow of energy within the sculpture. Remember the core, the pulsating heart of your creation. Use the techniques outlined in "Whispers of Light" to create subtle pulsations of light that emanate from the core and flow outwards, tracing the contours of the serpent's body. This will give the impression of an internal fire, a source of boundless energy that constantly animates the sculpture.

Crafting a Solar Serpent is more than just sculpting a form; it's about capturing the essence of a celestial being, its raw power, its inherent grace, its connection to the very heart of a star. It's a testament to the power of stardust sculpting, a demonstration of the artist's ability to harness the forces of the universe and shape them into something truly extraordinary. Each curve, each scale, each flicker of light tells a story of cosmic creation. The completed Solar Serpent, bathed in the light of a distant star, becomes a symbol of the artist's mastery, a tangible manifestation of the infinite potential that lies within the stardust from which we all are born. Remember, the true beauty of a Solar Serpent lies not just in its form, but in the sense of awe and wonder it inspires.

4.4 Asteroid Antelope

The Asteroid Antelope is no gentle grazer of cosmic plains. It is a creature of jagged edges and shimmering facets, a testament to the sculptor's ability to harness the raw power of asteroid belts. Imagine a creature born of shattered rock, pieced back together not with biological sinew but with threads of pure starlight. Begin by selecting asteroids of varying sizes and compositions. Iron-rich asteroids will lend a dark, metallic sheen to the antelope's hide, while those containing olivine or pyroxene can provide vibrant green and brown hues. Consider the interplay of light and shadow on these different surfaces, planning how they will contribute to the overall aesthetic of the creature.

The process of assembling the Asteroid Antelope requires a delicate balance of force and finesse. Gravitational tethers, carefully calibrated, can be used to draw the chosen asteroids into a central cluster. Think of these tethers as invisible strings, orchestrating a cosmic ballet. As the asteroids converge, use pulses of controlled energy to fuse them at their points of contact. Avoid complete melding; the antelope's form should retain a sense of fragmented beauty, a mosaic of celestial debris.

The antelope's horns, magnificent spirals of obsidian and nickel-iron, demand particular attention. These are not merely decorative appendages; they are symbols of the creature's untamed spirit. Carefully select elongated asteroid fragments, twisting them into elegant curves as they cool and solidify. Embed veins of shimmering gold or platinum along the horn's length, creating a visual representation of the powerful energies coursing through the creature. Consider the direction and angle of each horn, ensuring they convey a sense of dynamic movement, as if the antelope is perpetually poised to charge across the cosmos.

The body, a complex tapestry of metallic greys and earthy browns, should evoke both strength and fragility. Larger asteroids can form the core of the body, while smaller fragments create a sense of texture and detail. Leave gaps and crevices between the asteroids, allowing glimpses of the void to peer through, hinting at the emptiness from which the antelope was born. These voids can also be used to incorporate subtle lighting effects, further enhancing the creature's otherworldly presence.

Infuse the antelope with a sense of motion. Its legs, slender pillars of fused rock, should appear poised mid-stride. Tilt the body slightly forward, as if the creature is about to launch itself into the vast expanse of space. Consider the angle of the head and neck, adding a sense of alertness and curiosity. The Asteroid Antelope is not a static sculpture; it is a captured moment of cosmic dynamism.

The final touch involves imbuing the Asteroid Antelope with a subtle luminescence. Introduce trace amounts of radioactive elements within the asteroid fragments. This will cause the creature to emit a faint, ethereal glow, further emphasizing its otherworldly nature. The glow can be modulated to create different effects, from a gentle shimmer to a vibrant pulse, adding another layer of complexity to the artwork. This internal light source, emanating from the very core of the antelope, will create a captivating interplay of light and shadow, enhancing the textures and contours of its fragmented form.

Remember, the Asteroid Antelope is more than just a sculpture; it's a narrative crafted from the remnants of shattered worlds. It speaks to the power of creation from destruction, the beauty that can emerge from chaos. It embodies the sculptor's ability to transform the raw materials of the universe into something truly extraordinary. Each carefully chosen asteroid, each precisely placed fragment, contributes to the overall narrative. The Asteroid Antelope stands as a testament to the infinite possibilities of stardust sculpting, a vibrant symbol of the artist's vision and skill. Let your imagination run wild, explore the diverse textures and compositions of asteroids, and craft a creature that is uniquely your own. The universe is your canvas, and the stardust is your clay.

4.5 Void Wraith

The Void Wraith presents a unique challenge in stardust sculpting. Unlike the more tangible forms of the Cosmic Leviathan or the Asteroid Antelope, the Wraith deals with the ephemeral, the unseen, the suggestion of presence rather than solid form. It is a creature of pure shadow, woven from the deepest recesses of void dust, existing on the periphery of perception. To craft a Void Wraith is to sculpt absence, to give form to emptiness.

Begin by identifying a region of your workspace where light is weakest. This pocket of dimness will serve as the Wraith's anchor, the point from which its shadowy form will emanate. Don't be tempted to illuminate this area. Embrace the darkness, allow your eyes to adjust, and understand that the Wraith thrives in the unseen. This creature exists not in opposition to light, but in its absence. This delicate interplay is key to capturing its ethereal essence.

Gather the finest void dust, the particles that cling to the edges of nebulae, almost too fine to perceive. This dust, with its inherent darkness, is the Wraith's primary substance. Hold it gently within your cupped hands, feeling its subtle chill, its almost nonexistent weight. Imagine it not as a material to be molded, but as a darkness to be shaped, coaxed into a semblance of form.

Instead of directly shaping the void dust, focus on manipulating the light around it. Use strategically placed crystals or reflective surfaces to divert and absorb light, creating areas of deeper shadow within your designated dim space. These manipulated shadows will serve as the scaffolding for your Wraith. They form the negative space that defines the creature's form. Think of sculpting with light as an indirect approach to shaping the darkness.

As the shadows deepen, begin gently introducing the void dust into these darkened areas. Don't force it, let it drift and settle like smoke. Observe how the dust interacts with the manipulated light, how it absorbs and amplifies the shadows, giving them depth and texture. The Wraith's form begins to emerge not as a solid construct, but as a gradation of darkness, a whisper of presence.

The Wraith's movement is crucial to its character. It should not glide or float, but rather undulate and shift like a mirage, its edges blurring and reforming. To achieve this, subtly alter the placement of your light-manipulating tools. The slightest shift in a crystal's angle can cause the shadows to tremble and the Wraith to seemingly ripple and dissipate, only to coalesce again in a slightly altered form. The goal is to create a sense of constant, subtle motion, as if the Wraith exists in a state of perpetual flux.

Consider incorporating elements that hint at the Wraith's sentience. A faint shimmer within the deepest part of its shadow, perhaps achieved with finely ground moonstone dust, can suggest an inner light, a spark of awareness within the void. This subtle detail adds a layer of mystery and depth, inviting the viewer to contemplate the nature of this elusive being. The Wraith's power lies not in its physicality, but in its enigmatic presence.

The completion of a Void Wraith is not marked by a definitive form, but by a feeling. When you sense a presence in the darkness, a chilling awareness that something unseen observes you, then you have succeeded. The Wraith is not meant to be fully understood, but to be felt, a subtle shift in the atmosphere, a whisper in the stillness. It's the embodiment of the unseen, a testament to the power of suggestion in stardust sculpting.

Remember, the Void Wraith is a testament to the power of subtlety. It is a sculpture born of darkness, a creature of shadow and suggestion. It requires patience, a keen eye for the interplay of light and absence, and a willingness to embrace the unseen. The true artistry of the Void Wraith lies in its ability to evoke a sense of mystery, to whisper of the unknown, and to remind us that sometimes, the most powerful forms are those we cannot fully perceive. The void is not empty, it is full of potential, waiting to be shaped by the skilled hand of the stardust sculptor. The challenge is not to create something from nothing, but to reveal the something that already exists within the nothing. This is the essence of the Void Wraith. This is the art of sculpting absence.

5 Celestial Architecture

Imagine manipulating the fabric of spacetime itself, weaving quasars into shimmering domes. These structures wouldn't be built in the conventional sense, but rather coaxed into existence, harnessing the immense energy and gravitational forces of these celestial bodies. The dome's structure wouldn't be solid, but a mesmerizing interplay of light and energy, contained within a framework of warped space. Consider the potential for artistic expression: manipulating the quasar's light to create breathtaking displays within the dome, shifting colors and intensities to evoke different moods and emotions. Imagine stepping inside, enveloped by the hum of cosmic energy, the very air vibrating with the power of creation. This is the realm of Quasar Domes, where architecture transcends physical limitations and enters the realm of pure energy manipulation.

Think of comets, not as icy rocks trailing dust, but as the building blocks of grand cathedrals. These wouldn't be structures of stone and mortar, but soaring edifices of solidified cometary material, imbued with an otherworldly luminescence. Picture vast naves crafted from the icy nucleus, stained-glass windows formed from the shimmering dust tails, illuminated from within by captured starlight. Comet Cathedrals would be monuments to the ephemeral beauty of the cosmos, a testament to the artist's ability to harness the fleeting wonders of the universe and transform them into enduring works of art. Each cathedral could be unique, reflecting the distinct composition of its cometary source, a celestial fingerprint frozen in time. The challenge lies not only in shaping the cometary material, but also in preserving its delicate beauty, ensuring that the cathedral stands as a beacon of light against the backdrop of the infinite void.

Now, envision the moon's surface not as a barren landscape, but as the canvas for intricate labyrinths. These wouldn't be simple paths carved into the lunar dust, but complex, multi-layered structures that burrow deep beneath the surface. Imagine descending into a Lunar Labyrinth, the walls shimmering with captured starlight, the path winding through a network of tunnels and chambers. Each turn could reveal a new marvel: a cavern filled with bioluminescent lunar flora, a chamber echoing with the whispers of captured solar winds, or a hidden grotto reflecting the light of distant nebulae. Lunar Labyrinths wouldn't merely be structures; they would be journeys of discovery, invitations to explore the hidden depths of the moon and the artist's imagination.

The construction of these architectural wonders presents a unique set of challenges. Working with celestial bodies requires an understanding of their unique properties and behaviors. Quasar Domes demand mastery over gravitational forces, the ability to manipulate the very fabric of space. Comet Cathedrals necessitate a delicate touch, a deep respect for the fragile beauty of cometary material. Lunar Labyrinths call for an intimate knowledge of the moon's geology, an ability to carve and shape its subterranean world.

The scale of these projects is immense, requiring a vision that transcends earthly limitations. Building with stardust isn't about simply piling materials; it's about harnessing the energy and essence of the cosmos. It's about weaving together light and gravity, transforming celestial bodies into works of art.

Consider the artistic possibilities: imbuing Quasar Domes with pulsating light shows, orchestrating the colors of cometary dust within a Cathedral's nave, creating hidden gardens within the depths of a Lunar Labyrinth. The potential for expression is as boundless as the universe itself.

This form of celestial architecture isn't about creating permanent structures, but rather about capturing the ephemeral beauty of the cosmos. These structures would exist as fleeting masterpieces, eventually succumbing to the relentless forces of the universe. Their transience adds to their allure, reminding us of the ever-changing nature of reality.

This isn't just about building structures; it's about creating experiences. Imagine wandering through a Quasar Dome, bathed in the light of a distant galaxy. Pic-

ture attending a celestial concert within a Comet Cathedral, the music resonating with the vibrations of the cosmos. Envision getting lost within a Lunar Labyrinth, discovering hidden wonders at every turn. These architectural marvels would be more than just structures; they would be gateways to otherworldly experiences.
Finally, consider the philosophical implications of celestial architecture. Building with stardust elevates the act of creation to a cosmic scale, blurring the lines between art and the universe itself. It invites us to contemplate our place within the vast expanse of existence, to see ourselves not as separate from the cosmos, but as integral parts of its grand design. This is the ultimate expression of art, a testament to the boundless creativity of the human spirit and the infinite wonders of the universe.

5.1 Quasar Domes

Imagine harnessing the raw power of a quasar, its energy swirling and contained within a shimmering dome of sculpted stardust. This is the essence of celestial architecture on a grand scale. Quasar domes are not mere structures; they are dynamic works of art, pulsating with captured energy, radiating light and warmth across the sculpted landscapes. Building such a structure demands a deep understanding of both cosmic forces and the artistic principles of form and function. We begin not with physical materials, but with the careful manipulation of gravitational fields, weaving together the fabric of spacetime itself to form the dome's underlying framework.
This framework, invisible to the naked eye, acts as a cosmic scaffolding, capable of containing the immense energies we intend to harness. Think of it as a carefully woven net of gravity, strong enough to hold the quasar's fiery heart. The next stage involves gathering nebular dust, the raw material of our dome. This isn't a simple process of collection; it requires a delicate dance with the cosmic winds, guiding the dust particles into the gravitational framework, allowing them to settle and coalesce. The density and composition of the dust will dictate the final dome's optical properties, its ability to refract and reflect the quasar's light, transforming it into a breathtaking display of celestial artistry.
As the nebular dust accumulates, it begins to interact with the contained quasar

energy. This isn't merely illumination; it's a transformative process. The energy excites the dust particles, causing them to shimmer and glow with otherworldly hues. Here, the sculptor's skill truly comes into play. By carefully modulating the energy flow, we can control the intensity and color of the light emitted by the dome, creating breathtaking patterns and visual effects. Imagine a dome that shifts from a cool cerulean blue to a vibrant violet, then pulsates with a warm golden glow, all orchestrated by the artist's manipulation of the quasar's energy. The structural integrity of a quasar dome is paramount. While the gravitational framework provides the initial support, it's the careful layering and compaction of the nebular dust that gives the dome its strength and resilience. We must consider not just the aesthetics, but also the physics of the structure. The dome needs to withstand the immense pressures exerted by the contained quasar energy. This is achieved through a process of celestial tempering, a technique involving the careful application of controlled bursts of stellar radiation. These bursts fuse the dust particles together, creating a solid, yet ethereal shell capable of containing the quasar's power.

The final stage is perhaps the most crucial. It's not enough to simply contain the quasar's energy; we must harness it. We achieve this by creating intricate networks of energy conduits within the dome's structure. These conduits, formed from specially treated stardust, channel the quasar's energy outwards, powering the surrounding celestial landscape. Imagine cities bathed in the soft glow of harnessed quasar light, or vast gardens flourishing under its life-giving energy. This is the true potential of a quasar dome, not just a work of art, but a source of power and life.

Consider the artistic possibilities. Imagine crafting a dome that projects intricate patterns of light across the landscape, transforming the night sky into a canvas for your celestial artistry. Or perhaps a dome that emits a soothing, harmonious hum, resonating with the very fabric of the universe. The possibilities are endless, limited only by the sculptor's imagination and skill. The creation of a quasar dome is an intricate dance between art and science, a testament to the boundless creativity that flourishes when we embrace the infinite canvas of the cosmos.

Each dome becomes a unique expression of the artist's vision, a beacon of light and

energy in the vastness of space. Furthermore, these domes are not static creations. They evolve and change over time, the nebular dust slowly swirling and shifting, creating an ever-evolving display of cosmic artistry. Imagine walking within the dome's luminous embrace, bathed in the quasar's light, feeling the subtle hum of its energy resonating through your very being. This is the experience of celestial architecture, a merging of art, science, and the infinite wonders of the universe.
The beauty of a quasar dome lies not only in its grand scale, but also in the intricate details. The play of light and shadow on the swirling nebular dust, the subtle variations in color and texture, the gentle hum of harnessed energy—all these elements combine to create a truly awe-inspiring experience. This isn't merely construction; it's a symphony of cosmic proportions. As you gaze upon a completed quasar dome, you are witnessing not just a structure, but a testament to the power of human creativity to harness the very forces of the universe and transform them into works of breathtaking beauty and profound significance.
Ultimately, the creation of a quasar dome is a journey of discovery, a process of pushing the boundaries of artistic expression and exploring the infinite possibilities of the cosmos. It's a testament to the human spirit's inherent desire to create, to innovate, and to leave its mark on the universe. It's an invitation to embrace the boundless potential within us all, to reach for the stars, and to sculpt our own otherworldly wonders from the stardust of our dreams. Every detail, from the curvature of the dome to the intricate patterns woven into its surface, reflects the artist's unique vision, transforming a functional structure into a powerful statement of creative intent.

5.2 Comet Cathedrals

Imagine the nucleus of a comet, a conglomeration of ice and dust, not as a scientific phenomenon, but as the keystone of an immense, ethereal cathedral. Its irregular form, riddled with crevices and shadowed hollows, becomes the foundation for a structure that defies earthly architectural conventions. We are not building with steel and stone, but with the very fabric of the cosmos. Consider the trails of vapor and dust, the comet's coma, as the nascent arches and flying buttresses of our celestial edifice. These wispy trails, illuminated by the distant sun, form shimmering, translucent vaults, creating an otherworldly play of light and shadow. This isn't construction; it's a cosmic dance, a delicate interplay between gravity and the solar wind, shaping our cathedral into a form both magnificent and ephemeral.

The comet's journey through the void becomes the narrative of our cathedral. As it approaches a star, the increasing heat sublimates the ice, intensifying the coma and tail. We harness this energy, sculpting the expanding trails into intricate spires and delicate traceries. The cometary dust, composed of microscopic grains of silicates, carbon, and even organic molecules, provides a palette of subtle hues—from the deep blacks of carbon to the shimmering silvers of silicates. Imagine manipulating these particles with focused beams of starlight, creating stained-glass windows of cosmic proportions. These windows wouldn't depict earthly scenes, but the swirling nebulae, distant galaxies, and the birth and death of stars—a testament to the grandeur of the universe itself.

Think about incorporating other celestial bodies into the design. Captured asteroids, rich in metallic ores, become the shimmering mosaics adorning the cathedral walls. Sculpt their surfaces with miniature comets, etching intricate patterns that reflect and refract starlight in a dazzling display. The faint light of distant nebulae could be channeled through strategically placed crystals, grown within the comet's icy heart, illuminating the cathedral's interior with an ethereal glow. The very structure would become a dynamic artwork, constantly evolving as the comet hurtles through space, its form and light show changing with its proximity to stars and other celestial bodies.

Now, envision the cathedral's interior. No solid floors or pews here, but swirling clouds of luminescent gas, shaped by carefully controlled magnetic fields. These gaseous formations serve as ethereal platforms, allowing visitors to float through the cathedral's vast interior, immersed in the symphony of light and color. Imagine sound sculptures created by the interaction of solar winds with the comet's magnetic field. These wouldn't be earthly melodies, but the whispers of the cosmos, resonating through the cathedral's airy spaces, a constant reminder of the universe's vastness and our place within it. The core of the comet, now a sacred chamber, could house a pulsating nebula, captured and contained within a sphere

of sculpted stardust. This celestial heart would beat with the rhythm of the universe, a source of both light and wonder, the focal point of our comet cathedral.
Consider the implications of scale. This is not a structure confined by earthly limitations. Our cathedral could span millions of miles, its spires reaching out into the void, dwarfing even the largest planets. Imagine the perspective of a visitor, floating among the comet's icy stalactites, gazing out at the swirling tapestry of stars and nebulae. This experience wouldn't just be visual, but a profound, spiritual journey, a direct communion with the universe itself. Construction, in the traditional sense, is irrelevant here. We are not building, but orchestrating, guiding cosmic forces to create a masterpiece of ethereal architecture. The comet cathedral becomes a testament to our ability to harmonize with the universe, to transform raw cosmic materials into a work of art that transcends earthly boundaries and inspires awe in all who behold it. It's a testament to the boundless creativity that arises when we embrace the infinite canvas of space. The cathedral's transient nature only adds to its beauty, a reminder of the ephemeral nature of existence and the preciousness of each fleeting moment. It's a fleeting masterpiece, a testament to the ephemeral beauty of the cosmos, a cathedral built not for eternity, but for a breathtaking, incandescent moment in time. The very act of creation becomes an act of worship, a celebration of the universe and our place within its grand design.

5.3 Lunar Labyrinths

The ethereal glow of partially formed lunar landscapes beckons. We've gathered our nebulae, tempered our void dust, and mastered the ephemeral. Now, we turn to architecture on a grand scale, a scale only the moon's desolate beauty can truly contain. Lunar labyrinths, complex and captivating, offer a unique challenge, a fusion of artistry and engineering. Unlike terrestrial architecture bound by gravity and material limitations, lunar labyrinths leverage the low gravity and unique properties of stardust to achieve breathtaking, gravity-defying structures. Think of swirling pathways that ascend into the lunar sky, interconnected arches that seem to float effortlessly, and vast, open chambers bathed in the soft luminescence of captured starlight.
Consider the possibilities of manipulating the lunar regolith itself. Imagine carv-

ing deep trenches into the surface, then lining them with luminous stardust, creating glowing pathways that snake across the lunar landscape. These pathways could lead to central chambers sculpted from compressed void dust, offering panoramic views of the surrounding lunar terrain. Picture these chambers adorned with intricate carvings, reliefs depicting celestial events or abstract patterns formed from the play of light and shadow. The very dust of the moon becomes our chisel, the starlight our illumination.

One might even incorporate elements of previously learned techniques. Recall the phantom textures from "Ethereal Forms." These could be used to create illusory walls and doorways within the labyrinth, adding an element of surprise and mystery. Perhaps a seemingly solid wall shimmers and disappears as you approach, revealing a hidden passage bathed in the soft glow of nebulae gathered from distant galaxies. The interplay of real and imagined spaces adds another layer of complexity to the labyrinthine experience. Think of the labyrinth not just as a structure, but as an experience, a journey through a dreamscape made real.

As we design our lunar labyrinth, we must consider the unique environment. The extreme temperature fluctuations, the constant bombardment of micrometeoroids, and the vacuum of space all present unique challenges. However, these challenges also offer opportunities. The extreme temperature differences can be utilized to create thermal currents, powering kinetic sculptures within the labyrinth. Micrometeoroid impacts, carefully channeled, could create shimmering patterns on exposed surfaces, adding an ever-evolving element to the design. The vacuum itself allows for the creation of enclosed environments with unique atmospheric conditions, perhaps filled with swirling nebulae or bathed in the otherworldly glow of captured starlight.

Don't restrict yourself to conventional notions of architecture. The low gravity of the moon allows us to create structures that defy earthly limitations. Imagine spiraling towers that reach towards the stars, connected by delicate bridges of spun stardust. Envision vast, open courtyards where sculptures crafted from ephemeral light dance in the lunar vacuum. Think of incorporating the lunar landscape itself into the design, weaving the labyrinth through existing craters and valleys, creating a harmonious blend of art and environment. The possibilities are as vast as the cosmos itself.

Let's consider the narrative potential of a lunar labyrinth. Imagine a path that winds through a series of chambers, each dedicated to a specific celestial event. One chamber might depict the birth of a star, another the collision of galaxies, yet another the slow, graceful dance of orbiting planets. The labyrinth becomes a journey through cosmic history, a story told in stardust and light. Each turn reveals a new wonder, a new chapter in the ongoing saga of the universe.

Remember the starseeds from "Stellar Gardens"? Incorporate elements of living sculpture within the labyrinth. Imagine pathways lined with bioluminescent lunar flora, casting an ethereal glow on the surrounding structures. Perhaps a central chamber houses a pulsating heart of living stardust, radiating warmth and light throughout the labyrinth. The integration of life into the architecture adds a dynamic, ever-changing element to the design.

Consider the interplay of light and shadow. On the moon, shadows are stark and unforgiving, but they can also be powerful tools for artistic expression. Design your labyrinth to utilize the long lunar shadows, creating dramatic contrasts and highlighting the intricate details of your sculptures. Imagine a towering archway casting a long, elegant shadow across a courtyard filled with delicate stardust sculptures. The interplay of light and darkness adds a layer of depth and mystery to the labyrinthine experience.

The creation of a lunar labyrinth is a monumental undertaking, but the rewards are immeasurable. It is a testament to the boundless potential of human creativity, a symbol of our enduring fascination with the cosmos. It is an invitation to explore the universe within, to wander through the landscapes of our dreams, and to discover the infinite possibilities that lie beyond the horizon. As you embark on this journey, remember the lessons learned, from gathering nebulae to shaping void dust. Embrace the challenge, let your imagination soar, and create a lunar labyrinth that will stand as a testament to the power of art in the face of the infinite.

6 Landscapes of Dreams

Imagine a canvas vast and dark, speckled with the faintest glimmer of nascent stars. This is the starting point, the raw material for crafting a landscape born of dreams. We begin with twilight nebulae, ethereal clouds of stardust swirling in the cosmic void. Unlike the vibrant, fiery nebulae bursting with newborn stars, these are quiet, contemplative spaces, their light subtle and diffuse. Think of the soft glow of dusk on a winter's evening, the hushed stillness just before nightfall. Capture this essence, this tranquility, in your nebula. Work with the finest particles of stardust, allowing them to drift and coalesce into diaphanous veils of color. Layer these veils, one upon another, creating depth and complexity. Hint at hidden forms within the nebula, shadowy suggestions rather than clearly defined objects. Let your intuition guide you, allowing the nebula to evolve organically, as if forming itself from the whispers of the cosmos.

These twilight nebulae serve as the backdrop for our dream landscape, a foundation upon which to build further wonders. Consider the emotional impact of your chosen palette. Deep blues and violets evoke a sense of mystery and introspection, while softer pinks and lavenders hint at serenity and wonder. Experiment with subtle shifts in color, creating gradients that mimic the slow, graceful dance of light through a nebula. Imagine how starlight might filter through these clouds, casting ethereal glows and creating pockets of luminescence. By mastering the interplay of light and shadow, you can imbue your nebulae with a sense of depth and atmosphere that draws the viewer into the heart of the dream.

Now, let us turn our attention to the creation of crystal canyons, dramatic formations carved from stardust solidified into crystalline structures. Imagine towering spires of amethyst and emerald, their facets catching and refracting the light of the twilight nebulae. Visualize deep chasms, their walls lined with shimmering quartz crystals, pulsating with an inner light. These canyons are not merely geological features; they are expressions of energy, solidified manifestations of the dreams that shape this landscape. To achieve this effect, consider the structure of your crystals. Sharp, angular formations suggest dynamism and power, while smoother, rounded crystals evoke a sense of tranquility and ancient wisdom.

The formation of these crystal canyons requires a different approach than the ethereal nebulae. Here, precision and intention are key. Begin by shaping the larger structures, the towering cliffs and deep ravines. Then, layer in the smaller details, the individual crystals that adorn the canyon walls. Pay close attention to the way light interacts with these surfaces. Imagine the sparkle of sunlight on a freshly fallen snowdrift, the way light refracts through a prism, creating a rainbow of colors. Replicate these effects within your crystal canyons, using light and shadow to accentuate the textures and forms. Experiment with different types of crystals, each with its own unique properties and visual effects.

As you sculpt these crystalline structures, think about the stories they tell. Perhaps the canyons were formed by ancient rivers of starlight, their paths etched into the very fabric of the landscape. Or maybe the crystals themselves hold memories, whispers of forgotten dreams and ancient prophecies. Infuse your creations with these narratives, allowing them to resonate with a deeper meaning. The interplay between the nebulae and the canyons is crucial. Imagine how the soft, diffuse light of the nebulae might filter through the crystalline structures, creating a mesmerizing display of color and light. Picture the shadows cast by the towering spires, adding an element of mystery and intrigue to the landscape.

To enhance the dreamlike quality of your landscape, consider incorporating elements of surrealism. Perhaps a river of liquid moonlight flows through the canyon, its surface shimmering with an otherworldly glow. Or maybe giant, bioluminescent flowers bloom on the canyon walls, their petals unfolding in slow, graceful movements. Don't be afraid to experiment with unexpected combinations of form and color. The goal is to create a landscape that transcends the boundaries of reality, a place where the laws of physics bend to the whims of the

imagination.
As you work, remember that the most important tool at your disposal is your own imagination. Allow yourself to be guided by your intuition, to explore the uncharted territories of your inner world. The landscapes of dreams are not bound by the constraints of the physical world. They are expressions of the soul, tangible manifestations of the intangible. By embracing this freedom, you can create truly unique and unforgettable works of art. Let your creativity flow, and allow your dreams to take shape in the stardust. The result will be a landscape that is not only visually stunning, but also deeply personal and emotionally resonant. It will be a testament to the power of imagination, a window into the infinite possibilities of the human mind. And finally, it will be a landscape that truly captures the essence of dreams.

6.1 Twilight Nebulae

Imagine a canvas vast and dark, speckled with the faintest glimmer of distant starlight. This is the starting point, the raw material for crafting a twilight nebula. Unlike the vibrant, energetic nebulae bursting with star formation, twilight nebulae are the quiet aftermath, the fading embers of cosmic creation. Their beauty lies in subtlety, in the gentle gradients of light and shadow, the wisps of dust and gas illuminated by the ghosts of departed stars. Creating these ethereal landscapes requires a different approach, a focus on nuance and the interplay of darkness and light.
Begin by selecting a region of your cosmic canvas. Consider its overall shape and the placement of any existing celestial bodies. Twilight nebulae often occupy the spaces between brighter objects, acting as a bridge or a backdrop, enhancing the overall composition of your stardust landscape. Think of them as the quiet moments in a symphony, the pauses that give meaning to the crescendos. Remember, negative space is just as important as the nebula itself. It frames the artwork, allowing the eye to rest and appreciate the subtle details.
Now, introduce the first layers of nebular dust. Work with fine particles, allowing them to drift and settle like cosmic snow. Focus on creating variations in density, allowing some areas to remain almost transparent while others become slightly

more opaque. This will give the nebula depth and a sense of three-dimensionality. Imagine the dust motes catching the faint light of distant stars, creating a hazy luminescence that shifts and changes as you move through the landscape. Think of the way fog hangs in a valley at dawn, obscuring and revealing in equal measure.

Introduce a limited color palette. Muted blues and purples, tinged with hints of grey and deep crimson, work well to evoke the fading light of a dying star. Avoid bright, saturated colors, as these will detract from the ethereal quality of the nebula. Instead, focus on creating subtle transitions between shades, allowing the colors to blend and merge seamlessly. Think of the subtle hues of a twilight sky on Earth, the way the colors shift and change as the sun dips below the horizon.

Next, consider the light sources within your nebula. Perhaps a dying star, a distant galaxy, or even the faint glow of a nearby nebula can provide the illumination. Position these sources strategically, allowing their light to filter through the dust and gas, creating highlights and shadows that define the nebula's form. Remember that light in space travels in straight lines, so pay attention to the way it interacts with the varying densities of the nebula. Imagine a lighthouse beam cutting through the fog, revealing the swirling mists and hidden shapes within.

To further enhance the depth and complexity of your twilight nebula, incorporate wispy filaments and tendrils of gas. These can be created by carefully manipulating the flow of stardust, creating delicate strands that seem to dance and weave through the nebula. These filaments add a sense of movement and dynamism, suggesting the slow, graceful currents that exist within these celestial clouds. Think of the delicate veins in a leaf, the intricate patterns they create on the surface.

Remember the importance of contrast. While twilight nebulae are inherently subtle, they are not entirely uniform. Introduce areas of greater density and opacity, creating dark, shadowy regions that contrast with the more luminous parts of the nebula. This interplay of light and shadow is crucial for creating a sense of depth and dimension. Imagine the way moonlight filters through the branches of a tree, creating dappled patterns of light and shadow on the ground below.

Finally, consider the overall composition of your twilight nebula within the larger context of your stardust landscape. Does it act as a backdrop for other celestial objects? Does it bridge the gap between different regions of your artwork? By carefully considering the placement and interaction of your twilight nebula with other elements, you can create a harmonious and evocative celestial tableau. Think of the way a painter uses different colors and textures to create a balanced and engaging composition.

Creating a twilight nebula is a delicate dance between light and shadow, a study in subtlety and nuance. By mastering these techniques, you can craft ethereal landscapes that evoke the quiet beauty of the cosmos, capturing the fading embers of creation and the infinite possibilities that lie within the darkness.

6.2 Crystal Canyons

The wind whispers secrets through these crystalline canyons, a song of creation echoing off facets sharper than any earthly blade. Light refracts and dances, painting the canyon walls with an ever-shifting kaleidoscope of color. Constructing such a landscape requires a delicate balance—a fusion of raw power and meticulous precision. Begin by visualizing the desired form. Imagine the sweep of the canyons, the towering spires, the delicate arches bridging the chasm. This mental blueprint will be your guide throughout the process.

Next, gather your stardust. For crystalline structures, a nebula rich in silicon and oxygen provides the ideal base. The specific composition will influence the final color and refractive properties of the crystals, so careful selection is crucial. Collect the nebula into a dense cloud, compressing it gently to initiate the crystallization process. This is a slow, deliberate process, akin to nurturing a delicate flower. Rushing the process can result in brittle, flawed crystals, shattering the illusion of timeless beauty.

As the stardust coalesces, guide its growth with carefully placed whispers of energy. Imagine these whispers as gentle nudges, encouraging the crystals to form along the contours of your mental blueprint. This process demands patience and a deep understanding of the material. Observe the way the light plays across the forming surfaces, adjusting your energy flow to maximize brilliance and clarity. The goal is to create a natural, organic flow within the canyon, mimicking the forces that shape landscapes on terrestrial planets.

Consider the interplay of light and shadow. Deep within the canyons, where starlight struggles to reach, introduce luminescent stardust to create pools of ethereal light. These glowing accents will contrast with the sharp, crystalline edges, adding depth and mystery to the landscape. Experiment with different intensities and colors of luminescence to create a dynamic and engaging visual experience. Imagine a soft, blue glow emanating from the canyon floor, contrasting with the fiery orange light refracted through the crystalline spires above.

The scale of your crystal canyons can vary dramatically. A miniature canyon, nestled within a cupped hand, can be just as captivating as a sprawling vista stretching across a vast expanse of space. The key is to maintain a sense of proportion and balance within the chosen scale. Intricate details, such as miniature crystalline flowers blooming along the canyon walls, can add a touch of delicate beauty to a larger piece. Conversely, a smaller canyon might benefit from a single, perfectly formed crystal acting as a focal point.

To enhance the realism of your crystalline canyons, incorporate elements of erosion and weathering. Imagine the relentless flow of cosmic winds, slowly shaping the canyon walls over eons. Recreate this effect by subtly etching the crystal surfaces, creating a sense of age and history. A dusting of cosmic dust, strategically placed, can further enhance the illusion of a natural, evolved landscape. Consider the effects of time on terrestrial rock formations—the smooth curves carved by flowing water, the jagged edges chipped by wind and ice. Emulate these patterns in your stardust sculptures to create a sense of depth and authenticity.

Finally, remember that the true beauty of your crystalline canyons lies not only in their visual splendor but also in the story they tell. Infuse your creation with emotion and meaning. Let the canyons whisper tales of ancient cosmic events, of the birth and death of stars, of the endless dance of creation and destruction. Each facet, each spire, each shadow should contribute to the narrative, creating a landscape that resonates with the viewer on a profound level.

Imagine the story of a meteor shower, captured in the crystalline structure of a canyon wall. The fiery trails, frozen in time, tell a tale of cosmic energy and dramatic celestial events. Or perhaps the canyons themselves are formed from the shattered remains of a celestial body, the jagged edges a testament to a cataclysmic past.

By carefully considering these elements, you can craft crystalline canyons that transcend mere sculpture and become portals to otherworldly realms. They will be landscapes of dreams, whispering secrets of the universe and inviting the viewer to embark on a journey of imagination and discovery. These canyons will be a testament to your artistry, a testament to the power of stardust to capture the infinite beauty of the cosmos.

7 Infinite Canvas

Imagine the universe as a vast, untouched canvas, stretching beyond comprehension. We, as stardust sculptors, have the privilege of shaping this celestial fabric, molding nebulae and coaxing constellations into existence. Our tools are not chisels and hammers, but whispers of energy and the gentle caress of gravity. This infinite canvas invites us to transcend the limitations of terrestrial art, to create wonders that defy the laws of physics and ignite the imagination. This is where the true magic of stardust sculpting lies: in its boundless potential, its capacity to reflect not only the external universe, but the inner universe of the artist.

Consider the sculptor's heart, the wellspring of inspiration from which all creation flows. It is a microcosm of the universe itself, filled with swirling emotions, nascent ideas, and the echoes of ancient starlight. Every sculpture, every ethereal landscape, is a reflection of this inner world, a tangible manifestation of the artist's dreams and aspirations. To truly embrace the infinite canvas, we must first delve into this inner space, exploring the depths of our creative potential. This introspective journey is not merely a philosophical exercise, but a crucial step in the artistic process. It allows us to connect with the universal energy that flows through us, the same energy that birthed the stars and galaxies.

This connection, once established, becomes the driving force behind eternal evolution. Our art, like the universe itself, is never truly finished. It is in a constant state of flux, transforming and refining itself with every passing moment. Each new creation informs the next, building upon previous experiences and pushing the boundaries of what is possible. Embrace this continuous evolution, for it is the lifeblood of the infinite canvas. Resist the temptation to become stagnant, to cling

ingness to surrender to the creative flow, allowing the universe within to guide your hand.

Imagine the delicate beauty of a lunar bloom, thriving in the seemingly barren landscape of the moon. This delicate flower symbolizes the resilience of the creative spirit, the ability to find beauty and inspiration in the most unexpected places. Cultivate this resilience within your own heart. Embrace the challenges that arise in the creative process, not as obstacles, but as opportunities for growth and discovery. Just as the lunar bloom draws sustenance from the seemingly barren lunar soil, so too can you draw inspiration from the challenges you face, transforming them into the fuel for your artistic endeavors.

Visualize the intricate architecture of a comet cathedral, its spires reaching towards the infinite expanse of space. This celestial structure represents the aspiration of the artist, the desire to create something that transcends the limitations of time and space. Nurture this aspiration within your own heart. Don't be content with merely replicating the forms of the physical world. Strive to capture the essence of the cosmos, the underlying principles that govern the universe. Let your sculptures be a testament to the boundless potential of human creativity, a reflection of the infinite possibilities that lie within the sculptor's heart.

Picture the ethereal beauty of twilight nebulae, their colors shifting and swirling in an otherworldly dance. These celestial landscapes represent the dreams and visions that reside within the artist's heart, waiting to be brought to life through the medium of stardust. Embrace these dreams, no matter how fantastical they may seem. Allow yourself to be transported by the power of your imagination, to explore the hidden depths of your inner universe. The more you connect with this inner landscape, the more authentic and compelling your artistic expressions will become.

Consider the crystalline canyons, their surfaces reflecting the light of distant stars. These landscapes symbolize the clarity of vision that comes from deep introspection. Cultivate this clarity within your own heart. Take time to reflect on your artistic journey, to examine the motivations and inspirations that drive your creative endeavors. The deeper your understanding of yourself and your artistic purpose, the more powerful and meaningful your sculptures will become.

The sculptor's heart is a microcosm of the universe, a space where infinite possibilities await to be discovered. Embrace the power of your inner cosmos, and let your sculptures become a testament to the boundless beauty and wonder that reside within. Remember, the true masterpiece is not the finished sculpture, but the journey of creation itself, the ongoing evolution of the sculptor's heart. It is in the continuous exploration of this inner space that we truly unlock the infinite potential of stardust and transform the whispers of infinity into tangible works of art.

7.2 Eternal Evolution

The universe is not static; it breathes, expands, collapses, and reforms. This constant flux, this eternal evolution, is the lifeblood of stardust sculpting. It is not enough to merely shape the void dust into a desired form; we must imbue it with the dynamism of the cosmos itself. Think of the slow, majestic spiral of a galaxy, the explosive birth of a star, the gentle drift of nebulae. These are the forces that shape our universe, and they should also shape our art. Embrace the concept of change, of growth, of decay. Allow your sculptures to tell a story not just of a moment in time, but of a process unfolding across eons.

Consider the implications of incorporating actual celestial movement into your work. A sculpture that slowly rotates, mirroring the spin of a distant planet. A mobile of shimmering nebulae that gently shifts and rearranges itself with subtle air currents, reflecting the chaotic dance of particles in space. A crystalline structure that refracts starlight in ever-changing patterns, simulating the passage of time through a cosmic lens. These are just a few examples; the possibilities are as limitless as the universe itself.

Furthermore, explore the concept of interconnectedness. No celestial body exists in isolation. Stars influence planets, planets affect moons, and everything is bathed in the cosmic radiation of distant quasars. Reflect this interdependence in your art. Create sculptures that interact with each other, that respond to each other's presence, that form a dynamic ecosystem of celestial forms. Imagine a cluster of crystalline structures that resonate with each other, their light and energy flowing back and forth in a mesmerizing display. Or perhaps a group of

sculpted astral creatures, each subtly influencing the movement and behavior of the others, creating a complex and evolving narrative within the artwork itself.
Don't limit your exploration to physical movement. Consider the evolution of form, of texture, of meaning. A sculpture crafted from a material that slowly changes color over time, reflecting the aging of a star. A surface that gradually erodes, mimicking the weathering of a celestial body by cosmic winds. These subtle transformations add another layer of depth and meaning to your work, inviting viewers to contemplate the passage of time and the impermanence of all things.
This principle of eternal evolution extends beyond the individual sculpture to encompass the entire artistic process. Be willing to experiment, to iterate, to abandon old ideas and embrace new ones. Don't be afraid to let your art evolve organically, guided by intuition and inspiration. View each creation not as a finished product, but as a stage in an ongoing journey of exploration and discovery. The universe itself is constantly changing, and so too should our artistic vision.
Remember, the true power of stardust sculpting lies not just in creating beautiful objects, but in capturing the essence of the cosmos itself. By embracing the concept of eternal evolution, you can imbue your work with a sense of wonder, dynamism, and profound meaning. Think about the grand cycles of creation and destruction that govern the universe. A nebula collapses to form a star, the star burns brightly for millions of years, then explodes in a supernova, scattering its remnants across space to form new nebulae, and the cycle begins anew.
Incorporate this sense of cyclical transformation into your work. Perhaps a sculpture that appears to be constantly reforming itself, shifting between different states of being, reflecting the continuous cycle of birth, death, and rebirth. Or a series of interconnected sculptures that represent different stages in the evolution of a celestial body, from its initial formation to its ultimate demise.
Engage with the inherent unpredictability of the cosmos. Sometimes, the most beautiful and unexpected results arise from embracing chance and allowing the materials to guide the creative process. Experiment with techniques that introduce an element of randomness into your work. Perhaps allowing the flow of stardust to dictate the final form of a sculpture, or incorporating naturally occurring

imperfections in the materials to create unique textures and patterns.
This embrace of the unexpected mirrors the very nature of the universe, where chaos and order are intertwined in a delicate dance. By relinquishing complete control, you open yourself up to the possibility of discovering new and exciting artistic avenues. It is in this interplay between intention and chance, between control and surrender, that true creativity flourishes.
Ultimately, stardust sculpting is not just about manipulating materials, but about engaging with the fundamental forces that shape our universe. By embracing the concept of eternal evolution, you can elevate your art beyond mere representation and into the realm of profound cosmic expression. Let your sculptures embody the dynamism, the interconnectedness, and the ever-changing nature of the cosmos itself. In doing so, you will create works that resonate with the deepest mysteries of existence and inspire awe and wonder in all who behold them. This is the true art of sculpting with stardust: to capture the infinite within the finite, and to reflect the eternal dance of creation in the palm of your hand.

7.3 A Universe of Art

Consider the universe. Not just the swirling galaxies and radiant nebulae, but the vast emptiness between them, the unseen forces that shape and bind it all. This is your palette. Your clay. Your canvas. You are a sculptor of stardust, and your potential is as limitless as the cosmos itself. Forget the limitations of earthly materials, the constraints of gravity and time. Here, in this infinite studio, you command the very fabric of existence. Think of the void as negative space, a vital component of your composition, just as important as the celestial bodies you sculpt. It's in the interplay of presence and absence that true artistry emerges.
Stardust sculpting isn't merely about mimicking the forms we see in the telescopes. It's about capturing the essence of the cosmos, the underlying principles that govern its chaotic beauty. It's about translating cosmic phenomena into tangible, albeit ethereal, works of art. Imagine capturing the dynamic dance of a binary star system, its swirling energies frozen in a delicate balance of light and shadow. Or perhaps recreating the birth of a star, the fiery explosion of creation captured in a shimmering cloud of stardust. This is the power you wield. The abil-

ity to capture the fleeting moments of cosmic evolution and transform them into enduring expressions of art.

Consider the possibilities of manipulating celestial light. Bend starlight into intricate patterns, weave nebulae into luminous tapestries, sculpt constellations into breathtaking three-dimensional forms. Think beyond mere representation. Explore the emotional impact of light and shadow, the way they can evoke wonder, awe, and even a sense of the sublime. Imagine a sculpture that pulsates with the rhythm of a distant quasar, its light echoing the ancient heartbeat of the universe. Or perhaps a nebula crafted from captured starlight, shifting and swirling in response to the viewer's gaze. This is the art of capturing light, of transforming it from a passive element into an active participant in your creation.

Explore the unique textures of celestial materials. The smoothness of void dust, the crystalline structure of nebulae, the rough, fragmented surfaces of asteroids. Each material offers a distinct tactile experience, a new dimension to your artistic expression. Imagine running your hand across the surface of a sculpture forged from solidified nebulae, feeling the subtle vibrations of cosmic energy pulsing beneath your fingertips. Or crafting a delicate, lace-like structure from captured solar winds, its ethereal form shimmering with trapped starlight. These are the tactile possibilities of stardust sculpting, a realm where texture transcends mere visual appeal and becomes a tangible expression of cosmic forces.

Don't limit yourself to static forms. Explore the dynamic potential of your medium. Sculpt celestial bodies that orbit each other, create nebulae that expand and contract, build galaxies that spiral and collide. Embrace the inherent dynamism of the universe and translate it into your art. Imagine a sculpture of a supernova in progress, its expanding shockwave frozen in a moment of cosmic upheaval. Or perhaps a miniature galaxy, its swirling stars and planets eternally locked in a mesmerizing dance. This is the art of capturing motion, of transforming the static nature of sculpture into a dynamic representation of cosmic evolution.

Consider the interplay of scale. Craft miniature universes contained within a single sculpture, or build colossal structures that dwarf entire galaxies. The universe offers an infinite range of scales, and as a stardust sculptor, you are free to explore them all. Imagine holding a galaxy in the palm of your hand, feeling the weight of billions of stars condensed into a single, tangible object. Or stepping inside a nebula sculpted on a planetary scale, becoming immersed in its swirling colors and luminous depths. This is the power of scale, the ability to manipulate perspective and create truly awe-inspiring works of art.

Think about incorporating sound into your creations. Capture the celestial music of pulsars, the whispering winds of nebulae, the roar of colliding galaxies. Transform these cosmic sounds into an integral part of your artistic expression. Imagine a sculpture that emits the haunting melody of a distant quasar, its sound resonating with the ancient vibrations of the universe. Or perhaps a nebula that whispers secrets to those who listen closely, its ethereal voice echoing the mysteries of creation. This is the art of capturing sound, of transforming the silent language of the cosmos into an audible experience.

Finally, embrace the unexpected. The universe is a place of constant change, of unexpected discoveries and awe-inspiring phenomena. Allow yourself to be surprised, to be inspired by the unknown. Don't be afraid to experiment, to push the boundaries of your artistic vision. Perhaps you'll discover a new way to manipulate stardust, a new form of cosmic expression that no one has ever imagined before. This is the true essence of art, the pursuit of the unknown, the constant exploration of the infinite possibilities of the universe. In the grand tapestry of the cosmos, you are not merely an observer, but an active participant, a sculptor of stardust, shaping and molding the universe into your own unique vision of art.

7.4 Beyond the Horizon

Imagine standing at the edge of a newly formed nebula, its colors swirling before you like a cosmic painter's palette. You've mastered the techniques of gathering nebulae, shaping void dust, and even coaxing lunar blooms into existence. Now, you face the ultimate challenge: pushing your artistry beyond the known, beyond the comfortable, and venturing into the true infinite canvas of the cosmos. This isn't merely about creating another ethereal sculpture or a breathtaking celestial cathedral. This is about finding the whispers of infinity within yourself and letting them guide your hand as you mold the universe itself.

Consider the concept of negative space. In terrestrial sculpting, we often focus on the form we are creating, the positive space it occupies. But in the vastness of space, the negative space, the void between celestial bodies, holds just as much potential. Think of sculpting not just the form of a nebula nymph, but the emptiness that defines her contours, the cosmic winds that caress her form and give her the illusion of movement. This interplay between presence and absence, between form and void, opens up entirely new avenues for artistic exploration. Embrace the void, not as an obstacle, but as another medium, another brushstroke in your cosmic masterpiece.

Reflect on the nature of time. On Earth, we perceive time as linear, a constant forward march. But within the cosmos, time bends and stretches, warped by gravity and the sheer scale of the universe. A sculpture created from a dying star carries within it the weight of eons, a history etched into its very being. Consider incorporating this concept into your work. Perhaps a sculpture that evolves over millennia, slowly changing form as the light from distant quasars washes over it. Or a celestial garden where the life cycle of lunar blooms is accelerated, allowing you to witness the birth, growth, and decay of entire ecosystems within a human lifespan. Time becomes not just a constraint, but another dimension to be manipulated and explored.

Now, contemplate the very essence of light. Light isn't merely illumination; it is information, energy, the very fabric of reality. We've already explored techniques like "Whispers of Light," but consider pushing those boundaries further. Imagine sculpting with pure light itself, weaving intricate patterns of photons, creating holographic illusions that dance and shimmer in the void. Think about capturing the light from a distant supernova and using it to illuminate a crystalline canyon, imbuing its walls with the echoes of a star's dramatic death. Light becomes not just an element of your art, but the very medium itself.

Furthermore, explore the concept of interactivity. Your sculptures don't have to be static, unchanging objects. They can react to their environment, to the gravitational pull of nearby celestial bodies, to the cosmic radiation that permeates the universe. Imagine a comet cathedral that resonates with the passing of a comet's tail, its structure humming with celestial energy. Or a solar serpent that shifts and coils in response to solar flares, its scales shimmering with newfound brilliance. By incorporating interactivity, you create sculptures that are not just objects of beauty, but living, breathing extensions of the cosmos.

Finally, remember the importance of perspective. When working on such a grand scale, it's easy to lose sight of the human element. But even in the vastness of space, your art is ultimately an expression of your own unique perspective, your own interpretation of the universe. Don't be afraid to infuse your creations with your emotions, your dreams, your fears. A sculpture born of sorrow can be just as powerful as one born of joy. The universe is your canvas, but your heart is your brush.

Embracing these concepts, negative space, the manipulation of time, light as medium, interactivity, and personal perspective will allow you to push the boundaries of stardust sculpting beyond anything you've previously imagined. This isn't just about creating beautiful objects; it's about engaging in a dialogue with the universe itself, expressing your innermost self on a cosmic scale. As you venture beyond the horizon, remember that the only limit is your own imagination. The universe awaits your touch. Let your creativity soar amongst the stars, and sculpt wonders that will echo through eternity. The canvas is infinite, the possibilities endless. What will you create?

7.5 Whispers of Infinity

Imagine the universe as a boundless studio, a canvas stretching beyond comprehension. We, the sculptors, stand poised with stardust in our hands, ready to breathe life into visions previously confined to the whispers of our imagination. This realm of infinite possibilities invites us to transcend the limitations of earthly materials and embrace the ethereal beauty of the cosmos. We are not merely crafting objects; we are weaving narratives across the tapestry of existence. Each sculpted form becomes a stanza in the grand poem of the universe, a testament to the boundless creativity residing within us.

Consider the vastness of space, the swirling nebulae painted across the cosmic canvas. Within these celestial clouds lies the raw material of our dreams – stardust, the very essence of creation. It is from this ephemeral substance that we draw inspiration and form. We gather these cosmic particles, not with physical hands, but with the power of our intent, shaping them into forms that defy earthly limitations. Think of the delicate balance required, the subtle manipulation of cosmic energies to coax these ethereal particles into tangible forms. It's a dance between the tangible and intangible, a delicate interplay of will and cosmic forces.

Now, shift your focus to the interplay of light and shadow within your creation. Light, in its infinite variations, becomes our chisel, carving depth and dimension into our ethereal sculptures. A whisper of light glancing off a curve can transform a simple form into a breathtaking spectacle. Imagine sculpting a nebula, capturing its ethereal glow within a crystalline structure. How would light refract through its swirling mists, creating an otherworldly luminescence? The possibilities are as limitless as the universe itself. Every ray of light, every flicker of shadow, contributes to the narrative we are weaving.

Our work extends beyond mere aesthetics; it delves into the realm of experience. We are crafting not just objects, but entire environments, landscapes of dreams born from stardust and shaped by imagination. Picture a canyon carved from crystalline starlight, its walls shimmering with an inner radiance. What stories would echo within its depths? What secrets would its luminous facets reveal? We are architects of the impossible, builders of worlds where the boundaries between reality and dream dissolve into a seamless tapestry of wonder.

This process demands a shift in perspective, a departure from the conventional notions of art. We are not bound by the constraints of gravity or the limitations of earthly materials. Our canvas is the infinite expanse of space, our medium the very fabric of existence. Imagine sculpting a comet's tail, capturing its ephemeral beauty in a frozen moment of stardust. What forces would you harness to achieve such a feat? How would you imbue it with the sense of motion, the dynamism of its celestial journey? The answers lie not in textbooks, but within the whispers of your own imagination.

Reflect on the ephemeral nature of our creations. Just as stars are born and fade away, so too will our stardust sculptures eventually return to the cosmic void. But their essence, the stories they tell, the emotions they evoke – these will linger in the hearts of those who have witnessed their ethereal beauty. This transient nature adds a layer of poignancy to our art, a reminder of the preciousness of every moment. Consider a sculpture crafted from the fading light of a dying star. What story would it tell? What emotions would it evoke in its viewers? The ephemeral nature of such a piece would only amplify its beauty and significance.

Our journey as stardust sculptors is an ongoing exploration, a constant interplay between vision and creation. We are not simply manipulating materials; we are engaging in a dialogue with the universe itself. Each sculpture we create becomes a question posed to the cosmos, an invitation to explore the boundless mysteries of existence. Imagine sculpting a black hole, attempting to capture its immense gravity and enigmatic nature in a tangible form. What challenges would you face? How would you represent the unseen forces at play? Such endeavors push the boundaries of our understanding, forcing us to confront the very nature of reality.

As you embark on this journey, remember that the true masterpiece is not the finished sculpture, but the journey itself. The process of creation, the exploration of possibilities, the dialogue with the cosmos – these are the rewards that await the intrepid stardust sculptor. Embrace the unknown, allow your imagination to soar beyond the confines of earthly limitations, and let the whispers of infinity guide your hand. For in the realm of stardust and dreams, anything is possible. The universe awaits your touch, ready to be molded into wonders beyond comprehension. The only limit is the boundary of your own creative spirit.

www.ingramcontent.com/pod-product-compliance
Ingram Content Group UK Ltd.
Pitfield, Milton Keynes, MK11 3LW, UK
UKHW021437240125
4283UKWH00041B/646

9 798348 402815